Investigating
Depression and Bipolar Disorder

Library of Congress Cataloguing-in-Publication Data

Meisel, Abigail.
    Investigating depression and bipolar disorder: real facts for real lives / by Abigail Meisel.
      p. cm.—(Investigating diseases)
    Includes bibliographical references and index.
    Summary: "Provides information about depression and bipolar disorder, including treatment, diagnosis, history, medical advances, and true stories about people with the diseases"—Provided by publisher.
    ISBN 978-0-7660-3340-5
    1. Manic-depressive illness—Juvenile literature. 2. Depression, Mental—Juvenile literature. I. Title.
    RC516.M426 2010
    616.89'5—dc22

                                      2008050060

Printed in the United States of America

022010 Lake Book Manufacturing, Inc., Melrose Park, IL

10 9 8 7 6 5 4 3 2 1

To Our Readers:
We have done our best to make sure all Internet Addresses in this book were active and appropriate when we went to press. However, the author and the publisher have no control over and assume no liability for the material available on those Internet sites or on other Web sites they may link to. Any comments or suggestions can be sent by e-mail to comments@enslow.com or to the address on the back cover.

♻ Enslow Publishers, Inc., is committed to printing our books on recycled paper. The paper in every book contains 10% to 30% post-consumer waste (PCW). The cover board on the outside of each book contains 100% PCW. Our goal is to do our part to help young people and the environment too!

INVESTIGATING
DISEASES

Investigating
Depression and Bipolar Disorder
Real Facts for Real Lives

Abigail Meisel

Enslow Publishers, Inc.
40 Industrial Road
Box 398
Berkeley Heights, NJ 07922
USA

Table of Contents

What Are Depression and Bipolar Disorder?

Depression and bipolar disorder are imbalances in brain chemistry that affect mood, perception, and behavior. They are often referred to as mood disorders. Years ago, people born with these imbalances stood little chance of leading productive and healthy lives. However, since the 1960s, better understanding of the causes of depression and bipolar disorder—and a revolution in medications for psychiatric illness paired with psychotherapy—has made both conditions treatable.

WHAT ARE THE SYMPTOMS OF DEPRESSION?

Unfortunately, no blood test or brain scan can diagnose depression and bipolar disorder. Depression can be difficult to diagnose because it takes so many different forms. Common symptoms include persistent sadness, irritability, feelings of anxiety, loss of interest or pleasure in life, neglect of personal responsibilities or personal care, changes in eating habits, changes in sleeping patterns, fatigue, and loss of energy. Depression is different from bereavement, which is a type of intense grief caused by a severe loss, such as a death. In teens, symptoms of depression may include reckless or self-destructive behavior, such as using drugs or having multiple sexual partners. If left untreated, depression can be fatal, leading to suicide.

WHAT ARE THE SYMPTOMS OF BIPOLAR DISORDER?

Bipolar disorder is a mood disorder just as depression is. Mental health professionals classify it in the same category of mood disturbance as depression. However, bipolar disorder combines two abnormal mood states: major depression and an intense excitement called mania. Symptoms of the mania can include a range of behaviors from wild spending sprees and sexual promiscuity to irritability. People with this condition cycle back and forth between these two extremes, often with a calm period or "plateau" in between. The cycles can occur as frequently as every two weeks or as rarely as every few years.

HOW MANY PEOPLE SUFFER FROM DEPRESSION AND BIPOLAR DISORDER?

Bipolar disorder affects approximately 5.7 million American adults, or about 2.6 percent of the U.S. population age eighteen and older, each year. Symptoms of mild, chronic depression, called dysthymic disorder, affect approximately 1.5 percent of the U.S. population age eighteen and older in a given year. This figure translates to about 3.3 million American adults.[1] The median age of onset of dysthymic disorder is thirty-one.

More severe and disabling than dysthymic disorder is major depressive disorder. Major depressive disorder affects approximately 14.8 million American adults, or about 6.7 percent of the U.S. population age eighteen and older in a given year. It is the leading cause of chronic disability in the United States. While major depressive disorder can develop at any age, the typical age at which most people develop it is thirty-two.[2]

WHO GETS DEPRESSION AND BIPOLAR DISORDER?

Depression and bipolar disorder can be passed from one generation to the next through genes and are present in every race, ethnic, and social group. For reasons not wholly understood, major depressive disorder is more common in women than in men.[3]

Until the mid-1990s, only adults over age eighteen were diagnosed with bipolar disorder. As the twenty-first century neared, pioneers in psychiatry realized that children and teens, too, can suffer from bipolar disorder and began to treat them for the disease.[4]

ARE THESE DISORDERS CURABLE?

For the moment, there is no permanent cure for either depression or bipolar disorder; however, both are quite treatable. Unlike other medical conditions, though, such as diabetes or epilepsy, depression and bipolar disorder each bear a heavy stigma in our society, particularly bipolar disorder. The first steps to successful long-term treatment are self-acceptance and willingness to participate in counseling sessions. In addition, people with bipolar disorder or major depressive disorder usually take medication.

ARE THESE DISORDERS PREVENTABLE?

Depression and bipolar disorder are not preventable, but their severity and duration can be lessened. People with these disorders stand the best chance of stability if they are diagnosed quickly after the onset of the disease, if they work with a well-qualified psychiatrist and receive psychotherapy, and if they are prescribed the correct medications. Also important are a healthy lifestyle and ample and ongoing support from friends and family.

Introduction

While depression takes many different forms, common symptoms include persistent sadness and irritability.

Clinical depression and bipolar disorder were long thought to be the result of emotional or even spiritual problems. Once seen as a personal weakness, a "bad attitude," or just "being crazy," depression and bipolar disorder are now understood to be biologically based physical diseases, just like diabetes or epilepsy. "The more research that is done, the more the science convinces us that there is simply no reason to separate mental disorders from any other medical disorder," said Thomas R. Insel, Director of the National Institute of Mental Health, when he was describing a series of studies on the connection between depression and the physical functioning of the brain.[1]

Like other serious medical problems such as heart disease or cancer, bipolar disorder and depression affect many women, men, teens, and children throughout the United States each year. Although approximately 20 million American adults age eighteen and older (and 6 million children) are *diagnosed with* depression and bipolar disorder, such statistics reflect only a fraction of the true number of people who *endure* depression and bipolar disorder.[2] The majority of affected individuals are undiagnosed, because the symptoms of depression and bipolar disorder often are not clearly identified.

The word "depression" refers to many subgroups of mood disorder. There are more than a dozen categories of depression, ranging from those that are triggered only in winter, when natural daylight is limited, to suicidal depression. Bipolar disorder, too, includes several sub-categories of disease. So many variations of these conditions exist that the impact on individuals also differs widely.

Some people with depression and bipolar disorder lead happy, healthy, and productive lives. They are spouses, parents, writers, musicians, CEOs, and even psychiatrists. Many people with bipolar disorder, in particular, are outstandingly creative and productive. With medication, therapy, and support from friends and family, they thrive.

Yet, depression and bipolar disorder should be taken seriously, for they can eclipse hope and joy from human life suddenly and completely. Untreated depression results in 31,000 suicides and 1.4 million attempted suicides in the United States each year—conservative estimates.[3] These statistics are grim, but not hopeless. Scientists across the nation—in research labs at leading medical centers—have taken on the challenge of deciphering the genetic codes of mental illness and relieving much of the suffering that depression and bipolar disorder now cause.

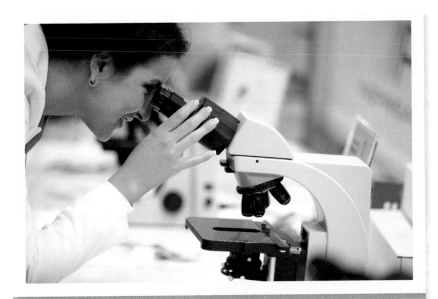

Scientists are working hard to uncover the biological causes of mental illnesses such as depression and bipolar disorder.

Straight Talk About Depression and Bipolar Disorder

THE DIAGNOSIS AND TREATMENT OF A TEEN WITH BIPOLAR DISORDER

Kyle Sorenson[*][1] pushed himself hard to excel at his passion, baseball. At six feet tall and 185 pounds, he was the starting pitcher on his Texas high school varsity team. In his sophomore year, Kyle's coaches encouraged him to aim for a college scholarship, especially because he also excelled academically. Then junior year arrived.

As the holidays drew near, Kyle felt strangely unenthusiastic, although he usually looked forward to both Thanksgiving and Christmas. He was sleeping more, and his fatigue wasn't simple tiredness; it was an intense exhaustion that overwhelmed him. The small irritations of daily life, such as lost homework or a disagreement with one of his parents or a classmate, made him so mad he could scream—and sometimes he did. The task of studying for his AP classes was almost too much to bear. Increasingly, he retreated to his room to watch television and play video games. His appetite vanished. Suddenly, his goals and dreams seemed worthless.

Kyle's parents noted the sudden change in his behavior. Alarmed, they called their family doctor, who recommended a consultation with a psychiatrist specializing in adolescents. For two hours the doctor took a detailed family history, speaking first to the Sorensons as a family, then just to Kyle's parents and, finally, to Kyle alone.

Kyle was surprised by what the doctor told him: Kyle's father's family was prone to bipolar disorder. Kyle's father's

* Not his real name

aunt and one of his older cousins took the medication lithium to control the condition. Kyle's father's grandfather may well have had bipolar disorder, too, the doctor said. The family history had revealed that he had been unable to hold down a job and that he had spent long periods of time away from his family, only to return home almost penniless.

The doctor explained that bipolar disorder was an imbalance in brain chemistry, causing alternating cycles of depression and mania, or "highs." She said that the condition often appeared in young adulthood and that the "down" phase generally appeared first.

During a manic phase, an individual with bipolar disorder might exhibit uncharacteristically exuberant behavior.

"I don't have enough information yet to make a diagnosis," the doctor told Kyle. "That might take more than a month. But I do know that mood disorders are treatable, and I promise that you will feel better once I can prescribe the right medication for you."

If Kyle were suffering simply from depression, she would recommend an antidepressant medication—but not in this case. "Antidepressants can trigger manic episodes. I want you to come for regular appointments so we can track what's going on with you," she said.

Kyle's "funk" continued for about two months. Then one weekend while out at a party with friends, his energy increased by tenfold.

"After months of feeling like a slug, I was suddenly a soaring eagle and stayed up and active for thirty-eight hours in a row," he recalled.

Continued on next page

Continued from previous page

"That was the first occurrence of mania for me," Kyle remembered. "In a weird way, it felt kind of good. Like I was invincible."

Kyle reported his abrupt change from agony to ecstasy to his psychiatrist. She asked him many probing questions: How many hours of sleep are you getting? Do you find yourself talking more quickly than usual? Do you feel a pressure to talk constantly? Have you been more sexually active than usual? Do you feel an urge to spend money?

Depakote can make a person gain weight, but it can also relieve bipolar symptoms very effectively.

On and on came the questions, and to each one Kyle answered "yes." Over the weekend, his friends kept telling him to slow down. At the party he went to, he found himself openly flirting with and then kissing a girl he barely knew, unusual behavior for him.

Finally, Kyle's psychiatrist had enough information to make a diagnosis. She wrote in her notes that day: *Patient is presenting with depression alternating with hypomania- Bipolar Disorder II.* Kyle's doctor recommended the medication Depakote to stabilize his moods. Depakote is a medication used for seizure disorders, migraines, and bipolar disorder.

Kyle's brush with mental illness changed the direction of his life—by adding a richer perspective. After an initial struggle, he accepted his mood disorder and the need for lifelong treatment. His psychiatrist and family adopted a "no shame" policy, encouraging Kyle's curiosity about his brain chemistry and his desire to be open about his condition with friends. When they noticed that Kyle had put on a few pounds after he began taking Depakote, he told his friends from school, "I'm not pigging out. The medication I take causes some weight gain."

Describing his mood disorder in a college essay, Kyle wrote: "If I had continued without diagnosis and treatment, I might have eventually lost my life to this disease. In a strange way I feel more human now, less invincible. Without the medical advancements of the last twenty years, my story would be a real tragedy, like that of my great-grandfather, from whom I inherited this condition. Now, I consider myself the hero of my tale, with a lot of love to support that success."

WHAT IS DEPRESSION?

Everyone feels sadness, melancholy, and even intense grief at some point in life because loss is an unavoidable part of the human experience. A friend or relative dies. A boyfriend and girlfriend break up. Parents divorce. There are tears, depression, and perhaps some anger, followed by emotional healing and a return to pleasure. For most people, this pattern will recur intermittently throughout life: a loss followed by a drop in mood and then a period of mending. For people suffering from major depression, moods have a life and a power of their own, separate from reality. They live in a bleak world in which each day is a struggle and the future holds no hope.

In describing the difference between grief and major depression, the author Kay Redfield Jamison writes: ". . . grief, fortunately, is very different from depression: it is sad but it is not without hope."[2] A majorly depressed individual lives without hope. He or she can have every outward appearance of success: a great career, a loving spouse and children, and financial security, yet still feel totally doomed and worthless. Depression is "cancer of the perspective."

No one knows exactly what triggers major depressive episodes in people. Scientists do know that there are three main causes of depression: problems with brain chemistry and an imbalance of brain chemicals called neurotransmitters; genes for the disorder, which are passed from one generation to the next; and an environment that is chronically stressful, such as one marked by extreme poverty or emotional, physical, or sexual abuse. War, too, is a trigger for depression as well as post-traumatic stress disorder, another emotional disability. A recent major study by the Rand Corporation (an organization devoted to researching and analyzing social trends) estimates that 300,000 veterans who served in either Iraq or Afghanistan are plagued by major depression or post-traumatic stress disorder.[3]

Scientists do know that there are three main causes of depression.

Depression is a public health crisis in the United States. The under-diagnosis and misdiagnosis of this condition are a "national disgrace," according to Lydia Lewis, president of the Depression and Bipolar Support Alliance, an advocacy group.[4] Depressive disorders affect approximately one in every eight teens and 2.5 percent of children below twelve years old.

BIPOLAR DISORDER

Bipolar disorder is a type of depression characterized by moods that "cycle" between mania ("highs") and depression ("lows"). Sometimes the mania of bipolar disorder is extreme, when people sometimes sleep for as little as three hours a night. Thoughts race through their mind at hyper-speed and one idea doesn't lead to the next. They can talk almost nonstop. Sometimes people who are experiencing mania feel that they are very powerful and important. At other times, they might feel extremely irritable and can explode into anger.

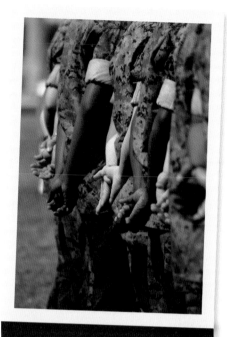

War can trigger both depression and post-traumatic stress disorder.

People experiencing what is called a manic episode are usually unable to continue functioning, either socially or in school or work, on a daily basis. In a manic state, a person may have a hard time understanding the difference between reality and fantasy. They can have hallucinations, hearing and seeing people and things that aren't really there. Sometimes people in a manic state will believe things that are not true, for example, thinking that they are a champion athlete or destined for stardom. The state of having hallucinations, delusions, or both is called psychosis.

In contrast to mania, hypomania (literally, "below mania") is a milder elevation of mood. Daily functioning is not impaired by this elation, although someone in this state frequently experiences a heightened sense of self-importance, greater energy and focus, and a speeded-up thought process. The range of mood between mania and hypomania is vast. Psychiatrists don't have a special word for every shade of

Bipolar Disorders and Creativity

For centuries, there has been an informal connection between a manic state and increased creative output. In her book *Touched with Fire*, Kay Redfield Jamison—a professor of psychiatry at Johns Hopkins University and world-renowned expert on bipolar disorder—argues that bipolar disorder and the artistic temperament are deeply related. According to Jamison, bipolar disorder (also referred to as manic depression) can inspire gifted people with an extra burst of energy, intellectual insight, and ambition—allowing them to achieve greater creative heights. Many of the world's most famous composers, artists, and writers are among the ranks of those who have mood disorders.

Vincent van Gogh, a nineteenth-century painter, experienced bursts of creativity in which he neglected all other activities so that he could focus on painting. These cycles of activity have led some to believe that van Gogh suffered from bipolar disorder.

Many well-known artists have suffered from bipolar disorder and been unbelievably productive during the manic cycles they experience. For example, the Dutch painter Vincent van Gogh created his canvases in "furies of painting" during which he neglected to eat or sleep.

mood, but they do divide the state of mania into "marked" (hypomanic), "severe" (manic), and "complete" (verging into psychosis).

There are three main types of bipolar disorder: Bipolar I disorder, Bipolar II disorder, and Bipolar disorder with rapid cycling.[5] All three are variations on the high-low mood cycle, with differences in degree of intensity and regularity of each state of feeling. People suffering from Bipolar I are more likely to experience hypomanias; for those with Bipolar II, the highs are less extreme and feel more like a burst of energy; and in Bipolar with rapid cycling, moods swing from high to low at more frequent intervals.

DEPRESSION AND BIPOLAR DISORDER IN CHILDREN AND TEENS

It's important to realize that major depression can affect children and teens as well as adults. Approximately 14 percent of people aged twelve to seventeen have experienced at least one physician-diagnosed episode of major depression.[6]

Although both teens and children can suffer from depression and bipolar disorder, these conditions look different in teenagers and in children under twelve than they do in adults. In children with bipolar disorder, there are no defined cycles of highs and lows. Moods ranging from hypomania to irritability to depression ripple through them, changing even within a single hour. Parents, teachers, and doctors often find the symptoms difficult to diagnose because they change so quickly. An estimated 1 million American children and teens have bipolar disorder.[7] The number of teens and children diagnosed with bipolar disorder has increased 600 percent in the last ten years as more research and information become available about the childhood form

Are Depression and Suicide Linked?

Left untreated, both depression and bipolar disorder can lead to suicide, but not in a majority of cases. According to the National Institute of Mental Health, suicide is a major public health problem in the United States. It is the eleventh leading cause of death overall and the third leading cause of death among young people ages eighteen to twenty-four, following accidents and homicides. Incidents of suicide have been increasing in our society, with non-Hispanic whites and Native Americans at highest risk. Almost four times as many males as females die from suicide.

of the disease. Still, many doctors think that bipolar disorder, like attention deficit hyperactivity disorder (ADHD) is over-diagnosed in children.[8]

Teens with bipolar disorder have a particularly rough road. Adolescence is a time of experimentation, testing boundaries, and finding an identity. Bipolar disorder can tip the risk-taking that is normal for adolescents into a high danger zone. For teens with bipolar disorder, the impulsive behavior, lack of sound judgment, heightened sexual energy, and irritability created by bipolar moods can be particularly dangerous, especially when they lead to illegal behavior like illegal drug use. According to the National Mental Health Association, an advocacy group devoted to promoting mental health across the United States, 75 to 80 percent of teens receiving inpatient substance abuse treatment have coexisting mental and emotional disorders.[9]

CAN PEOPLE WITH A DEPRESSIVE DISORDER OR BIPOLAR DISORDER LIVE A NORMAL LIFE?

Before the mid-1960s, there were no effective medications for bipolar disorder, but since then, a "biochemical revolution" has occurred. Mood disorders that once were regarded as life sentences can now be treated. Both depression and bipolar disorder have been considered manageable conditions since the 1970s. Depression is currently treated with one or more of a host of different medications to rebalance brain chemistry. Most of these medications fall into one of two groups: monoamine oxidase inhibitors (MAOIs) and selective serotonin reuptake inhibitors (SSRIs). Both of these groups of drugs reverse depression by attacking it at the level of nerve cells.[10]

For people with bipolar disorder, the most commonly prescribed drug is lithium, which came into use in the United States in the 1960s. Since then, other medications for bipolar disorder have been developed, and medications originally created for other conditions, such as epilepsy, have been adapted to treat patients with bipolar disorder successfully.[11]

A treatment plan includes medication, therapy, and lifestyle changes, including exercise and family support.

Ideally, depression and bipolar disorder are treated with a comprehensive plan that is overseen by a mental health professional. A treatment plan includes medication, therapy, and lifestyle changes, including exercise and family support. With a successful treatment plan implemented, people with both these conditions can lead long, productive, and even outstanding lives.

Comorbidities

A comorbidity is one disease or symptom that is related to another one and occurs at the same time. For example, people who suffer from depression often have other physical or emotional problems that accompany and can complicate their mood disorders. Alcoholism is now considered to be an emotional disorder, and belongs to the family of mood disorders that includes depression. Mood disorders coexist with alcoholism in many families; researchers have discovered that alcohol dependence and major depressive disorder are linked genetically. In fact, they have demonstrated linkage on the long arm of a specific chromosome, number 7.[12, 13]

Compulsive gambling is another problem that is seen side-by-side with certain types of depression. Compulsive gambling often mirrors the symptoms of bipolar disorder: Many gamblers act as though they are hypomanic when they are gambling. When they are losing, they can exhibit symptoms of depression. The spouses of compulsive gamblers frequently suffer from depression because they feel helpless as they watch the family's money being gambled away.

CELEBRITIES WITH DEPRESSION[14]

NAME	OCCUPATION
Britney Spears	Recording artist
Jim Carrey	Actor
Keisha Buchanan	Singer
Ben Stiller	Comedian and actor
Martin Lawrence	Stand-up comedian and actor
Sinéad O'Connor	Singer and actress
Winona Ryder	Actress
Sylvia Plath	Twentieth-century American poet
Owen Wilson	Actor
Larry King	Television personality
Kurt Cobain	Musician
Brooke Shields	Actress
Terry Bradshaw	Retired NFL quarterback and sportscaster
Abraham Lincoln	American president
Billy Joel	Musician
Ashley Judd	Actress

History of Depressive Disorders

P eople who suffered from major depression in the nineteenth century faced a very different fate than those who suffer today, especially when their behavior veered out of control. Regarded as inferior or flawed, they were frequently confined to institutions, or restrained in a straightjacket. A mere hundred years—just a pinprick on the timeline of humanity—separates people with mental illness who spent years incarcerated from those who are able to lead productive lives because of advances in the fields of psychiatry and in the development of psychiatric medications.

In fact, before about 1950, there was slim chance that a person with a major mood disorder could live a normal life. Before that time, mental illnesses were not seen as biologically based conditions. Instead, afflicted individuals were seen as weak (at best) or evil (at worst). The mentally ill were branded as "lunatics" because according to popular conception their behavior was ruled by the cycles of the moon. In fact, the word *lunatic* is derived from the Latin word for moon, or "luna."

"CONFINEMENT"

The census of 1840 marked the first attempt to collect data about mental illness in the United States.[1] In the 1870s, many professionals concerned with the fate of the mentally ill, including physicians, social workers, lawyers and public officials,[2] adopted a policy of removing them from society and placing them in institutions. They established a model for mental hospitals in the United States, "confining" anyone who showed an extreme form of behavior. There was little or no effective treatment available in these institutions, where living conditions were often terrible, even prison-like. Those slated for confinement included anyone who was violent, suicidal, or homicidal. In most cases, however, it wasn't a doctor or social worker who sought the confinement for a person: it was a family member. For example, between 1846 and 1847, 75 percent of all commitments to a typical U.S. mental hospital were initiated by family members.[3]

A Cruel Choice

Today, such practices seem harsh and inhumane. Who would abandon a loved one in a house of horrors? But, those were different times, before the birth of modern psychiatry and medications. Short of removing the mentally ill from the community, very little could be done to keep them safe from themselves and to protect others from their extreme behavior.

In the days before private and federal health insurance, an adult or teenager who couldn't work was seen as a drain on family resources. Most families could not afford doctors' bills or special treatments, and they needed every member to be productive in order to survive. In addition, mentally ill adults were universally rejected. They terrified their relatives and they brought disgrace to the family name.[4] No one understood them. No one wanted them around.

According to the U.S. census of 1880, America had a population of 50 million, including 91,997 "insane persons." This unfortunate group was 52 percent female, 71 percent native born, and 96 percent white.[5]

This 1912 postcard shows the entrance to the Utica State Lunatic Asylum in New York.

The Institution

Inside the hospitals for the mentally disabled, often called simply institutions, male and female inmates were separated by gender, sorted into like groups according to their symptoms, and herded into separate wards. There, they lived in subhuman conditions. This is why institutions were dubbed "snake pits, because they were terrifying and dangerous places to be."[6]

In 1890 a new law, the State Care Act, shifted the responsibility for the mentally ill of America to the state.

Effective psychiatric medications were still decades away, so physicians dosed the mentally ill patients with concoctions of their own making to keep them drugged and tranquil.

Among the institution population were not only the mentally ill, but also old people suffering from Alzheimer's disease or senility, the homeless, and epileptics.[7]

In 1890 a new law, the State Care Act, shifted the responsibility for the mentally ill of America to the state.[8] Legislators hoped that this new bill would force states to provide more and better care for their mentally ill populations. In truth, state-run institutions never truly improved or became places of healing for the men and women consigned to their care.

Diagnosing With the DSM

The *Diagnostic and Statistical Manual of Mental Disorders* (DSM-IV-TR, or the DSM for short), published by the American Psychiatric Association, is used by all mental health professionals to diagnose mental illness. The first edition of the DSM was published in 1952, with revised editions following through 2000.

Each version is upgraded as new research sheds light on mental disorders, and as society changes its view about what constitutes normal behavior. Homosexuality, for example, was listed in the DSM until 1973, when it no longer was tabulated among psychological disorders.

Mental health professionals must be highly trained to use the DSM properly because it is a complex text using a multidimensional approach that considers clinical symptoms, developmental disorders, physical condition (such as brain injury), severity of environmental stress (such as divorce or a sudden shock), and the highest level of functioning at the time of evaluation.

The DSM is to psychiatry what a playbook is to a football team. Without it, diagnosis would be a far more chaotic and less successful process.[9]

THE EMERGENCE OF PSYCHIATRY

What did progress was the field of psychiatry, which became an increasingly accepted medical specialty. In 1921, the American Medical-Psychological Association changed its name to The American Psychiatric Association (APA), which still exists as the premiere organization of psychiatrists in the United States.

Using data from the U.S. census and other sources, psychiatrists began classifying emotional disorders. They were starting to fully comprehend the frequency and complexity of these problems. They created work groups to study emotional disorders and to create scientifically based criteria for their diagnoses. The eventual result was the *Diagnostic and Statistical Manual of Mental Disorders*,[10] known among clinical professionals at the DSM. It is the bible of psychiatry.

As science superseded superstition in the field of mental health, doctors redefined their mission. Instead of confining the mentally ill to institutions, physicians tried to treat them with a variety of techniques, including the earliest form of talk therapy, called psychoanalysis.

SIGMUND FREUD

Developed by the eminent Viennese physician Sigmund Freud (1856–1939) at the start of the twentieth century, psychoanalysis was a technique for penetrating the deepest corners of the human mind, by talking. Freud believed that all mental and emotional problems—from those as severe as the brain disorder schizophrenia to milder ailments—could be traced to childhood conflicts. His method was straightforward. Patients reclined on a long couch in his office and "free associated," saying whatever came to mind. Gradually, themes would emerge from the hours of talk, enabling both

Sigmund Freud is known as the father of psychoanalysis.

doctor and patient to pinpoint the underlying causes of the psychological problem. Freud felt that this "talking cure" would uncover the conflicts at the root of his patients' troubles.[11]

Freud's method of psycho-
analysis became widespread
and even fashionable in
Europe and in the United States
during the early decades of the
twentieth century.

BIOLOGICALLY BASED THERAPIES AND TREATMENTS

Freud's method of psychoanalysis became widespread and even fashionable in Europe and in the United States during the early decades of the twentieth century. Freud's approach of attacking emotional problems with a "talking cure" was purely psychological. At the same time that Freud's theories gained popularity in the United States, other psychiatrists began exploring a very different approach to the treatment of emotionally based problems. This group of doctors argued that disabling emotional disorders were caused by structural or chemical malfunctions within the brain.[12] The idea that mental illness was essentially physical—like diabetes or heart disease—began to take root within the scientific community in the 1930s.

Biologically based treatments developed during that decade include insulin shock therapy, chemical convulsive therapy, electroconvulsive shock therapy, and lobotomy. The theory behind shock therapies was that they would deliver a radical jolt to the nerve cells in the brain, stabilizing its chemical imbalance. Lobotomy, a radical surgical procedure in which a section of the brain is severed, took a structural rather than chemical approach to the challenge of "fixing" a malfunctioning brain.

Insulin Shock Therapy

In the early 1930s, Manfred J. Sakel, a Polish neurophysiologist and neuropsychiatrist, discovered by accident that he could use the hormone insulin to treat patients suffering from psychosis (a state of mind characterized by hallucinations and delusions).

Insulin regulates blood sugar. Sakel accidentally gave a psychotic patient on overdose of insulin, causing a temporary coma and convulsions. The patient, who suffered from a mental illness called schizophrenia, improved for a time. This was the first medical attempt to treat schizophrenia, a brain disease that is still difficult to control. It was also the first attempt to treat diseased brains in this fashion, and shock therapy was also used in treating other disorders, such as depression.

Sakel continued the use of insulin shock therapy and reported that 70 percent of his patients improved.[13] Later studies showed that the treatment was not a real cure and that the improvements were temporary. Still, Sakel singlehandedly destroyed a centuries-old myth that schizophrenia was a curse rather than a biologically based disease.

The Chemical Convulsion Cure

Hungarian physician Ladislaus von Meduna, a contemporary of Sakel, noticed that schizophrenia was rare in epileptics. He also observed that when epileptics did have seizures, they seemed calmer afterward. He decided to trigger seizures in schizophrenics with a powerful drug called metrazol. Meduna was later criticized for experimenting on people with drugs. Yet his basic premise was correct: faulty "wiring" in the brain's nerve cells can be improved by physical means.[14]

Electroshock Therapy

Another product of the 1930s revolution in medical-psychiatric breakthroughs, electroshock therapy, produced convulsions in patients by delivering brief electric shocks to a part of the brain called the frontal lobe. Italian neurologist Ugo Cerletti revised the method, and as a result it gained popularity throughout the decade. Electroshock therapy proved safer and more acceptable to patients than chemical convulsive therapy.

This Ectonustim 3 ECT machine was used for electroconvulsive therapy. The photo also shows the electrodes that attached to the scalp.

Since its invention and use as a treatment for schizophrenia, it has also been used as therapy for severe, drug-resistant depression.[15] Electroshock therapy became a controversial treatment in the 1960s and 1970s, but it is currently accepted as an effective "last resort" in the treatment of depression and doctors have improved the way they administer the treatment to patients.

Lobotomy: The Surgical Treatment

Lobotomy is a surgical procedure on the brain intended to alleviate extreme mental or emotional problems. Lobotomy targets the frontal lobe. The procedure calms the behavior of extremely agitated or psychotic patients, making them docile by severing the link between the frontal lobes and the rest of the brain. The technique was developed in Europe by Dr. Antonio Egas Moniz, who won a Nobel Prize for his work in 1949.[16] Later, lobotomy was popularized in the United States by neurologist Walter Freeman and his colleague, a neurosurgeon named James Watts. First performed in the United States in 1937, the procedure was soon refined. Many saw it as a godsend and the solution to overcrowded institutions. Between 1939 and 1951, more than 18,000 lobotomies were performed in the United States.[17]

Lobotomy had serious consequences and drawbacks because of its effect on the emotions. To be "lobotomized" became a synonym in the popular culture for becoming an emotional robot, capable of little emotional response. Once again, researchers and physicians sought a nonsurgical cure to the seemingly insurmountable problem of mental illness. In 1952, a glimpse of hope appeared in the form of the drug chlorpromazine—a medicine that laid the groundwork for a revolution in the field of psychiatry.

What Is Lobotomy?

Before Thorazine was approved for the treatment of psychosis, a state of mind during which people experience hallucinations and delusions, doctors were desperate for a means of taming that frightening experience. The degree of their desperation is reflected in physicians' acceptance of lobotomy, now widely regarded as a barbaric procedure.

Lobotomy is the surgical cutting of white matter, the connective tissue that attaches the frontal lobes to the rest of the brain. The procedure gained great popularity in the United States during the 1940s when clinical neurologist Walter Freeman and neurosurgeon James Watts collaborated to create the Freeman-Watts Standard Procedure.

The surgery caught on but proved time-consuming, limiting the number of patients who could be operated on in a single day. In pursuit of a more efficient and profitable technique for severing the frontal lobe, Freeman adapted an Italian variation on the procedure and created the "ice-pick" lobotomy. He performed this operation after putting patients under local anesthetic. He made an opening at the top of the eye orbit and through it inserted a sharp tool into the brain, maneuvering it to sever the frontal lobe.[19]

Walter Freeman, the "ice pick lobotomist"

This version of the lobotomy provoked a backlash among the majority of physicians, who found it cruel. The procedure as a whole became dated by 1955, when Thorazine was approved for widespread use. Lobotomy lives on in classic American fiction, including the Ken Kesey novel *One Flew Over the Cuckoo's Nest*, a work that dramatizes the experience of being in a psychiatric ward during the heyday of lobotomy.

PSYCHOPHARMACOLOGY

By 1955, there were 559,000 Americans living in state psychiatric hospitals.[18] The nation desperately needed new ways to cope with the most extreme symptoms of mental illness, such as psychosis. Researchers at the American pharmaceutical company Smith Kline investigated reports that French psychiatrists were treating patients with a new drug called chlorpromazine. Smith Kline soon marketed the drug for use in U.S. state-run institutions. The results were spectacular. Patients who had been lost in a haze of psychosis were able to hold conversations and function with some degree of normalcy. In 1954, the U.S. Food and Drug Administration approved chlorpromazine for use.[20] Sold under the name Thorazine, it was used by approximately 50 million people worldwide by 1964.[21]

The success of Thorazine had an immediate impact on American society. In 1955, the number of patients admitted to psychiatric hospitals declined for the first time in a hundred years.[22] The government began to support research for medications to control medical illness. A new specialty within the field of psychiatry called psychopharmacology had been launched. This emerging area was devoted to researching medications to help mental illness and also to matching medications to individuals in order to obtain optimum results.

The Brain's Mood Centers

Crucial to the new field of psychopharmacology was an increased understanding of the mood centers of the brain. These mood centers rely on chemical compounds called neurotransmitters to carry messages between the brain's nerve cells. If there is a problem with neurotransmitters—if there are not enough of them or if they have a faulty structure—they fail to carry messages between nerve cells effectively. Mood suffers, and there is an onset of depression. There are more than a hundred different types of neurotransmitters, but the three that are most closely linked to depression are serotonin, norepinephrine, and dopamine. All the medications developed or discovered for the treatment of depression and bipolar disorder in the late 1950s through the 1990s work by improving the ability of neurotransmitters to carry messages successfully between nerve cells.

The success of Thorazine had an immediate impact on American society.

Medication Innovations

In the 1950s, researchers discovered two medications in addition to chlorpromazine that would prove extraordinarily significant. One was imipramine, later sold as Tofranil, a breakthrough drug in the treatment of depressive disorder. Tofranil improved the moods of people with depression and is part of a class of early antidepressants known as tricyclics.[23] This revolutionary medication was the by-product of an effort to find a new type of nonsedative allergy medication. Another lucky accident was iproniazid, the first entry in a new category of antidepressant called monoamine oxidase inhibitors (MAOIs).[24] Iproniazid was found during research for drugs to treat tuberculosis. Both of these drugs increased the amount of the neurotransmitter serotonin in the brain, alleviating depressed moods.

For people with bipolar disorder, called manic depression in the 1950s, the medication that would prove life-changing was a naturally occurring substance called lithium. Lithium is a metallic element, listed in the periodic table and used medicinally in the form of a salt or compound. Lithium was first used in Europe in 1949, but Americans waited until 1970, when the drug was approved for use in the United States, to receive the benefit of this medication.[25]

Taken in pill form, lithium calms the extreme mood swings of bipolar disorder, making everyday functioning possible. It eliminates both the "high-flying exuberance" and "black tiredness" of the cycle of bipolar disorder.[26] To this day, no one is sure exactly how lithium works because researchers are still trying to grasp the causes of bipolar disorder. Doctors agree, however, that lithium remains one of several valuable medications for stabilizing mood swings.

In the 1980s, the next generation of antidepressants, selective serotonin reuptake inhibitors (SSRIs), emerged to control depression. SSRIs were developed to raise levels of the neurotransmitter serotonin. SSRIs ensure that when the brain releases serotonin, it is not absorbed too quickly back into the nerve cells (neurons) during the process called reuptake. Because the SSRIs inhibit, or prevent, reuptake, they increase serotonin levels, which has been shown to improve mood.[27]

With the advent of Thorazine, the tricyclic antidepressants, MAOIs, SSRIs, and lithium, people suffering from schizophrenia, psychosis, and major depression could finally lead normal lives. But not all psychiatrists embraced these advances. With the rise of psychopharmacology, a rift appeared between Freudian psychoanalysts and a newer breed of psychiatrists, called biopsychiatrists. The old school of psychiatrists insisted that psychoanalysis was the only means of a long-term cure for mental illness.[28] Biopsychiatrists took a biologically based approach to treating mental illness. Doctors had to clear the "smoke" of mental illness with medications before they could begin to put out the "fire" of emotional problems with talk therapy. The tug of war between Freudian analysts and biopsychiatrists continued throughout the 1980s, but evidence about the effectiveness of medication mounted, and the older generation of psychoanalysts began to agree that medication had a valuable place in the treatment of numerous mental illnesses.

By the 1970s, the young psychiatrists emerging from medical schools and hospital residencies treated patients with depressive and bipolar disorders with a combination of medication and focused short-term therapy. Their goal was to reach out to patients in need, stabilize them with medication, and help them to lead independent lives. This model of care—the result of a hundred years' of painstaking research paired with an explosive growth of knowledge in the field of psychiatry—has given millions of Americans with major depression and other mental illnesses a chance at leading a successful life.

HOW REAL PEOPLE DEAL: KAY REDFIELD JAMISON

Thousands of students of psychiatry have learned about the diagnosis and treatment of bipolar disorder by reading the standard medical text on the topic, *Manic-Depressive Illness*, co-authored by Kay Redfield Jamison. Manic depression is an older term for bipolar disorder. Not all people realize, however, that Dr. Jamison, a professor of

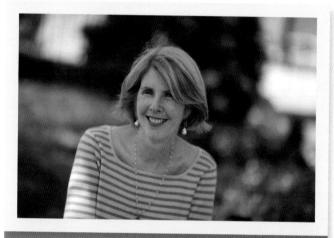

Doctor Kay Redfield Jamison is a pioneer in research on bipolar disorder and personally suffers from the disease.

psychiatry at the Johns Hopkins School of Medicine, knows what she writes about from firsthand knowledge as well as from academic training. Jamison experienced her first attack of manic-depressive illness, or bipolar disorder, when she was a senior in high school.

Her disorder brought her bursts of creativity and productivity intermingled with depression so severe she lacked the energy "to fill an ice cube tray." In her memoir *An Unquiet Mind*, Jamison describes the shopping sprees, violence, and attempted suicide that nearly derailed her life before she began taking the medication lithium as prescribed. Jamison has written two additional studies about the power of what she prefers to call manic depression: *Touched with Fire: Manic-Depressive Illness and the Artistic Temperament* and *Night Falls Fast: Understanding Suicide.*

She is one of the first American women to attain the status of full professor in academic psychiatry and the only known authority on bipolar disorder who can speak to the highs and lows of the condition with an insider's perspective.

The Science of Depression and Bipolar Disorder

D epression can have many causes, including environmental ones: stress, verbal or physical abuse, drug abuse, or poverty. Researchers now understand that prolonged exposure to any of these stressors can actually change the way the brain functions, thereby triggering depression. It is also true that someone can live in a safe and emotionally healthy environment and still become depressed because of a genetic predisposition to the condition. This is why four siblings can be raised in the same family and one might struggle with depression while the others do not. Clearly, those at highest risk for depression have "depression-prone" genes and also live in an environment that triggers a depressive reaction. The interplay between the biology of depression and external causes of depression is complex and still being studied.[1] Research of twins provides compelling data that depression is, indeed, genetically based. Although scientists have not yet found a single gene that points to depression, they do know that pairs of identical twins, who have identical genes, are more likely to both suffer from depression than sets of other siblings.[2]

BRAIN BASICS

The brain is the control center of the human body. The average brain weighs about 1,400 grams (three pounds). The human brain is the product of millions of years of evolution.[3] It guides people's most primitive acts (suddenly looking

Cerebrum

Parietal Lobe

Frontal Lobe

Occipital Lobe

Cerebral Hemisphere

Temporal Lobe

Limbic System (within)

Brain Stem

Cerebellum

This illustrated diagram identifies the various parts of the brain, which allow humans to perform tasks from sensing and responding to danger to calculating mathematical equations.

over a shoulder when they sense danger) to their most intellectually sophisticated ones (solving a calculus problem). Basic parts of the brain include the following:

- **The brain stem**—Also called the reptilian brain, the brain stem dates back 500 million years. It handles primitive functions, such as breathing and heart rate. It also alerts us to danger, even before the awareness of a threat becomes fully conscious.
- **The cerebellum**—Meaning "little brain," the cerebellum is attached to the brain stem and coordinates balance and the movement of our muscles. This part of the brain has more than tripled in size in the last million years.
- **The limbic system**—This "newer" region of the brain evolved approximately 200 million years ago. It is located in the center of the brain, immediately above the brain stem. In addition to maintaining heartbeat, body temperature, and blood pressure, the limbic system contains

two major glands that are important in regulating mood, the hypothalamus and the pituitary gland. The limbic system also regulates hunger, thirst, and other primary functions of the body. The limbic system responds to messages from senses and thoughts and is an important emotional processing center of the brain.

- **The cerebral hemispheres**—The brain can be divided into two halves called the cerebral hemispheres. Each half controls the opposite side of the body. This is why if someone has a stroke on the right side of the brain, the left side of the body is affected. Covering each hemisphere is a layer of nerve cells called the cortex.
- **The lobes**—The cortex gives humans the unique qualities of being able to organize, remember, and understand information. It is divided into four sections called lobes. The frontal lobe is involved in planning, decision making, and problem solving.[4] In humans, the frontal lobe doesn't develop fully until early adulthood, about age twenty-four. This is one of the reasons that adolescence can be a time of impulsive behavior and rocky judgment.[5] The parietal lobe is a perception center of stimuli related to touch, pressure, temperature, and pain. The occipital lobe controls many aspects of vision, and the temporal lobe is linked to hearing and memory.[6]

A HIVE OF COMMUNICATION

The brain is a center of communication for the entire body. All day long, rapid-fire chemical messages zip between nerve cells. The brain has approximately 100 billion of these nerve cells, or neurons.[7] With so many nerve cells in the brain, it's easy to envision them packed side by side like sardines, but the opposite is true. The neurons in the brain do not exactly touch. For one to communicate with another, one neuron must release a chemical messenger—the neurotransmitter—into a narrow passageway between the two cells called a synapse. The receiving nerve cell is like a magnet, attracting the neurotransmitter onto its surface. The neurotransmitter then binds with receptors on the outer coating of the receiving nerve cell. Once the receiving nerve cell gets the message, it sends the neurotransmitter back into the synapse, where it waits for a signal to reunite with the sending neuron. This reuniting process is called reuptake. Back in the sending neuron, the neurotransmitter is either stored or broken down by monoamine oxidase enzymes.[8] (These are the same enzymes that play a role in the action of monoamine oxidase inhibitors, a type of medication used to treat depression.)

The brain has approximately 100 billion nerve cells, or neurons.

NEUROTRANSMITTERS AND MOOD

What does all this activity have to do with mood? Everything. Physicians and researchers believe that insufficient neurotransmitters or a blip in the process of reuptake can plunge someone into a major depression. They cannot fully explain why neurotransmitters are so critical to mood, but the link between the two is indisputable and has provided one of the keys to understanding why major depressions emerge in people.[9]

Three types of neurotransmitter that researchers have consistently linked to mood are serotonin, norepinephrine, and dopamine. A deficiency in any of these brain chemicals spells trouble for maintenance of mood. Advanced brain imaging studies called positron emission tomography (PET) scans can show the activity of the normal brain, the bipolar brain, and the depressed brain. The scan of the depressed brain looks like a neighborhood at night, with just one or two street lamps lit.

It's a gloomy expanse with one or two bright spots. The normal brain has entire streets lit up; there's a balance between light and dark. The manic brain is lit up like Times Square, ablaze with electrical activity.[10]

HORMONES AND MOOD

When people are depressed, neurotransmitters aren't the only biological element involved. Brain areas that are involved in mood include the thalamus and the hypothalamus. The thyroid and the adrenal glands (not in the brain) are also involved, all of which secrete hormones that regulate parts of our lives that are commonly disturbed during episodes of depression: appetite, sleep, sexual desire, and memory.[11] Depression is a whole-body experience.

The Thyroid

The thyroid is a small butterfly-shaped gland that sits at the base of the front of the neck. The gland takes iodine from food and converts it into thyroid hormone. Our bodies need thyroid hormone to control metabolism—the conversion of oxygen and food into energy for cells. Every cell depends upon the proper functioning of the thyroid to survive. When the thyroid is out of balance and working too sluggishly (hypothyroidism), depression can take over.[12] This is why people suffering from depression are often tested for a deficiency in thyroid function.

The Hypothalamus

The thyroid is part of a system of glands that are ultimately controlled by the hypothalamus, located at the core of the brain. The hypothalamus regulates the secretion of hormones, including stress hormones. When you sense a threat, your hypothalamus sends a signal to your adrenal glands to secrete the hormone adrenaline into your bloodstream to rapidly prepare your body for an emergency situation. This is known as a fight-or-flight response. Repeated episodes of this fight-or-flight reaction can trigger depression because continual release of adrenaline disrupts the natural chemistry of the brain. This is why repeated exposure to actual and perceived threats—whether they're wartime battles or the angry shouts of an alcoholic parent—can tip someone toward depression. Psychiatrists link post-traumatic stress disorder (PTSD), which is frequently experienced by soldiers returning home, to continual activation of the fight-or-flight response and also to depression.[13]

Sex Hormones

Sex hormones such as progesterone and estrogen are also undoubtedly linked to mood. For example, premenstrual women commonly experience a change in mood, involving depression and irritability. When the mood change is severe, the condition is called pre-menstrual dysphoric disorder (PMDD). Once thought to be a normal part of the menstrual cycle, PMDD is now regarded as a psychiatric issue that affects 3 to 8 percent of all women. Another hormone-related mood disorder is postpartum depression, also called postpartum blues. When a woman is pregnant, her levels of estrogen and progesterone—female sex hormones—gradually increase. Then, in the twenty-four hours after birth, the levels of these hormones drop rapidly. Plummeting hormone levels can cause feelings from mere irritability to sadness, profound despair, and even suicidal thoughts.[14]

Repeated episodes of this fight-or-flight reaction can trigger depression because continual release of adrenaline disrupts the natural chemistry of the brain.

HOW REAL PEOPLE DEAL: BROOKE SHIELDS'S POSTPARTUM DEPRESSION

Brooke Shields has been a public figure since she was a baby featured in Ivory Snow ads. She has been the star of both television shows and movies and is the mother of two small children. After the birth of her daughter, Rowan, Shields experienced an unexpected postpartum depression. Despite the fact that many hospitals educate new mothers about the signs of postpartum depression, Shields found that she was totally unprepared for the major depression she suffered when her daughter was a newborn. Shields detailed her experience in her memoir, *Down Came the Rain: My Journey Through Postpartum Depression*. In July 2005, Shields wrote an opinion piece in the *New York Times* describing her experience with postpartum depression. "At my lowest points, I thought of swallowing a bottle of pills or jumping out the window of my apartment," Shields wrote. She credits antidepressant medication combined with therapy with saving herself and her family.

Shields ended her essay by pleading with pediatricians to take a moment to talk to new mothers about postpartum depression when they are in the office for check-ups instead of focusing solely on the baby.[16]

Brooke Shields wrote a book about her battle with postpartum depression.

Because hormones are related to mood—and because women experience greater shifts in hormone balance each month—women experience depression more often than men. When boys and girls enter adolescence, they have the same rate of depression, but by age fifteen, young women are twice as likely to have a major depressive episode.[15] Most physicians and researchers look to hormones to explain this gender gap. According to the American Academy of Family Physicians, this trend extends into adulthood. Women experience depression twice as often as do men. However, men who are depressed are at greater risk for substance abuse and for suicide.[17]

TYPES OF DEPRESSION

The number of variables that can play a role in causing depression is staggering: neurotransmitters, monoamine oxidase enzymes, the responses of the limbic system, the thyroid and adrenal glands, and sex hormones—all have been studied and are considered important keys to understanding depression. Just as these biological origins of depression are widely varied, so, too, are the types of depression people experience. Depression is really an umbrella term for a series of related mood disorders. Depression has been studied and categorized extensively in order to differentiate one type of the condition from another. This is important for accurate diagnosis and treatment. Some of the most common subcategories of depression include:

Seasonal affective disorder is a type of depression that is sparked by the shortened amount of daylight in the fall and winter months.

- Dysthymia—The mildest form of depression
- Major depressive disorder
- Depression during or after pregnancy
- Recurrent depression
- Seasonal affective disorder (SAD)—Caused by decline of daylight hours in the fall and winter.[18]

What is "Parity" in Mental Health?

The brain is a part of the human body, but until recently, brain-based disorders, such as depression, have been regarded by society and by health insurance companies as emotional rather than physical in nature. As a result, someone with a history of bipolar disorder or another depressive disorder might be denied insurance coverage for visits to the type of specialist they need to see: a psychiatrist.

Congress passed a bill requiring insurance companies to provide mental health insurance "parity" for problems like addiction and depression.

In March 2004, the House of Representatives passed a bill requiring insurance companies to provide mental health insurance "parity" for problems like addiction and depression. This means that health insurance companies must cover treatment for these brain-based disorders just as they do for diabetes, heart disease, cancer, and other diseases of the body.

The concept of parity is a complicated one. Some people with major mood disorders have them for life and will not be treated for a given period of time and then experience a recovery. Should an insurance company be expected to pay for life care? What about diagnosis? There is no blood test for bipolar disorder and an accurate diagnosis might take months. Should an insurance company pay for all the therapy sessions leading to diagnosis? Parity introduces a greater sense of fairness into the health insurance system, and it acknowledges that people with mental disorders need medical care. As Congress continues the debate over parity, millions of Americans wait eagerly to see if their physically based emotional disorders will receive the treatment they need.[19]

WHO GETS DEPRESSION?

Sometimes people become temporarily depressed because of external (environmental) circumstances: They are grieving a death, experiencing a divorce within a family, or grappling with a big disappointment. In major depression, there may be no environmental factor that triggers the depression.

Depression is a cross-class problem. Being more affluent or of a certain racial or ethnic background doesn't lessen or increase chances of depression. Here's what does: People who have primary family members (a parent or sibling) with depression are seven percent more likely to experience depression. People who have a primary family member who is an alcoholic are eight percent more likely to experience depression.[20] Other risk factors include: introversion, insecurity, stress sensitivity, and dependency as personality traits. Lack of intimate relationships is another common risk factor.[21]

THE UPS AND DOWNS OF BIPOLAR DISORDER

Bipolar disorder is a separate category of depression in which an elevated mood (either mania or hypomania, a less severe form of mania) is followed by depression and then by mania once again in "cycles." Symptoms of mania include wildly inflated self-esteem, pressure to keep talking, sexual promiscuity, and decreased need for sleep, perhaps only two to three hours a night.

Cycling can occur as often as once every few days and as infrequently as every few years. In children, bipolar disorder is far less stable and mood swings can occur several times an hour. As a result, researchers and psychiatrists are still creating a model of what bipolar disorder looks like in someone under age twelve.

CAUSES OF BIPOLAR DISORDER

Bipolar disorder is less common than depression. Both men and women are equally at risk for bipolar disorder, which statistically has been shown to most commonly first emerge in teens or young adults. Of approximately 18 million American adults with mood disorders, approximately 5.7 million have bipolar disorder.[22] It is a highly hereditary disease, meaning that there is a strong genetic component to the disorder. No one has pinpointed an exact cause of bipolar disorder, but researchers are actively targeting areas such as the endocrine (gland) system, neurotransmitters, disturbances in the natural rhythm of the body (circadian rhythms), and childhood stressors. These, in addition to a genetic predisposition to the condition, may make a person more vulnerable to developing a full-blown bipolar disorder.

A PIONEER IN BIPOLAR DISORDER RESEARCH: DR. KIKI CHANG

The biology of the human brain, classification of mood disorders, and theories of personality types are all interesting to study, but what good do these studies actually do? In real life, when a psychiatrist is trying to help a patient, he or she relies on years of training based on understanding brain chemistry, types of mood, and personality. Ideally, psychiatrists don't just write prescriptions, but are also able to use words powerfully to communicate with patients to help them overcome obstacles. Some psychiatrists contribute to their field by working as researchers in laboratories and striving for new breakthroughs. One of these researchers is Kiki Chang, MD.

Dr. Chang is an Associate Professor of Psychiatry and Behavioral Sciences at the Stanford University School of Medicine, Division of Child Psychiatry, and Lucile Packard Children's Hospital at Stanford, where he is the director of the Pediatric Bipolar Disorders Program. There, he spe-

Dr. Kiki Chang is an expert in the study of bipolar disorder.

cializes in treating children and adolescents for bipolar disorder. Dr. Chang has won many prestigious awards for his work and has received a five-year Career Development Award from the National Institutes of Health. As the program's director, Dr. Chang conducts research into various facets of bipolar disorder. He uses brain imaging to find out which of his patients might have a predisposition to bipolar disorder. He then uses medications and/or family therapy to see if he can delay the full onset of the disorder by starting to treat it before it truly develops, particularly in children of affected parents.[23]

A Teen With Major Depressive Disorder

Courtney[24] was sixteen and had been treated for ADHD for two years because teachers saw "problems with attention." During her sophomore year in high school, her grades began to drop, and her parents noticed that she was losing interest not only in academics but also in her friends and hobbies.

By the time she entered her junior year, Courtney's condition had grown increasingly worse. The pediatrician who prescribed Courtney's ADHD medication attributed Courtney's difficulties to the need for a higher dose of Ritalin, a drug commonly prescribed for ADHD. He increased her dose. Soon afterward, Courtney began showing classic symptoms of depression: She lost weight, had little energy, and seemed to take no pleasure in life. Still, her parents were reluctant to admit that their daughter might be depressed. For them, it was easier to accept that Courtney had ADHD than a mood disorder. Finally, in the middle of her junior year, Courtney announced that she was quitting high school. She couldn't think about going to college, she told her parents. She could barely get out of bed, take a shower, and eat. In the last six months, she'd lost twenty pounds, dropping from a size eight to a size four, without trying. Finally, her alarmed parents took Courtney in for a psychiatric evaluation. Courtney's symptoms were so apparent and severe that the doctor suggested she be put on an antidepressant medication right away. The psychiatrist told Courtney's parents that it was almost a miracle that she'd survived for a year feeling that bad. He prescribed Wellbutrin, an antidepressant that also often helps ADHD. Courtney was back on track within two weeks, and she later graduated from her high school in the top 20 percent of her class. She went on to a small liberal arts college—her original plan—and still takes her antidepressant medication daily.

Identifying Depression and Bipolar Disorder

D epression is a condition that takes many forms and can suddenly appear in people from children to senior citizens. It is the tenth most common diagnosis made during visits to family physicians.[1] If you took a snapshot of America's mental health on a given day, you'd see approximately one in four American adults has been treated for a form of depression from dysthymia (mild depression) to major depression. One in eight American teenagers suffers from major depression.[2] Major depressive disorder is the leading cause of disability in the United States for people ages fifteen to forty-four.[3] It affects approximately 14.8 million American adults or 6.7 percent of the U.S. population age eighteen or older. The average age of onset is thirty-two years old.[4]

Depression appears differently in adult males and females.

Sometimes depression is like a primary color: It is easy to identify correctly at first glance. In about 45 percent of cases though, depression is like a subtle blending of two or more colors.[5] It is mixed with anxiety, a drug addiction, or an eating disorder, for example, to create a more complex variation of mood disorder. Mixed medical problems, including mood problems, are called comorbidities. They are harder to diagnose and to treat because they are more complex.

Depression not only takes an emotional toll on people and their families but costs the nation money. According to a study conducted at Johns Hopkins University in 2000, businesses in

Major depression affects one in eight American teenagers.

the United States spent $83.1 billion that year for costs associated with depression, including payment for employee health care, lost wages caused by missed work, and decreased workplace productivity.[6]

Depression appears differently in adult males and females. Depression has traditionally been considered to be twice as common in females as in males, and technically, that is true. However, doctors now feel that some of the root causes of depression, such as routine abuse or exposure to trauma, express themselves differently in men and women. Women tend to develop depression, while men often express anger and veer toward antisocial behaviors (such as committing crimes) or substance abuse.[7]

TEENS AND DEPRESSION

Depression also looks different in adults compared to teenagers. Angry and irritable feelings affect 85 percent of adolescents suffering from depression—a figure far higher than for adults.[8] A variety of other symptoms and behaviors, called depressive equivalents, are seen in teenagers that are not seen in adults and children. There is also a higher rate of suicide among teenagers suffering from depression. In fact, suicide is the third leading cause of death among teens.[9] Finally, teens are less likely than adults to follow through with their treatment plan, putting them at greater risk for harm.

CHILDREN UNDER TWELVE

Children younger than teens can experience a full range of psychiatric disorders; symptoms have been documented in children as young as two or three. However, there is a lot of

Can Bipolar Disorder Affect Children?

In the past decade, the number of children under age thirteen diagnosed with bipolar disorder has increased by 600 percent.[10] Although the disorder has been diagnosed in adults for close to a century, it was never thought to be a pediatric or childhood illness. In fact, doctors believed that bipolar disorder never emerged before the teenage years or young adulthood. All this changed in 1999 with the publication of a new book on the topic, *The Bipolar Child: The Definitive and Reassuring Guide to Childhood's Most Misunderstood Disease* by Demitri Papolos, MD, and Janice Papolos. The Papolos team argued that bipolar disorder was not rare in children and that, in fact, it was more common than doctors had ever envisioned and was frequently misdiagnosed. According to Dr. Papolos, children labeled with a host of other disorders—from attention deficit hyperactivity disorder (ADHD) to separation anxiety disorder and obsessive compulsive disorder—were actually bipolar.[11] The book provoked a sensation in the world of child psychiatry. Many disagreements among physicians followed, with some even accusing pharmaceutical companies of trying to create a new market for their medications by funding research about pediatric bipolar disorder. The debate continues about the prevalence of bipolar disorder among children under age thirteen.

controversy in the field of child psychiatry not only about what symptoms constitute a proper diagnosis but also about which treatments are the most appropriate for children. Psychiatric medications may have side effects for adults. For children, whose bodies are still developing, these medicines need to be monitored even more carefully. In addition, parents, teachers, and even

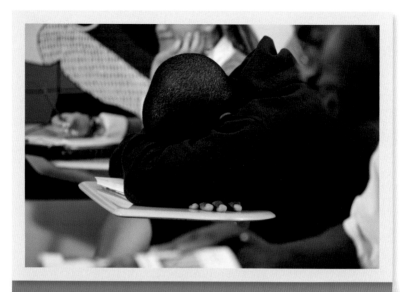

Stubbornness and defiance are not psychiatric disorders, and should not be mistaken for depression.

doctors can have a hard time distinguishing between psychiatric and developmental problems. A child might simply be defiant or stubborn by nature and not mentally ill.[12]

SYMPTOMS OF DEPRESSION AND BIPOLAR DISORDER

A diagnosis of major depression is contingent on a list of symptoms that must occur for at least two weeks without stopping (as opposed to situational depression). These symptoms may include: depressed mood, loss of interest or pleasure in normal activities, unintentional weight loss or gain, insomnia or hypersomnia (sleeping too much), fatigue, feelings of worthlessness or guilt, diminished ability to think or concentrate, and recurrent thoughts of death or suicide.

Bipolar disorder is very difficult to diagnose. Typically eight years pass between the first episode of depression or manic symptoms and the first medical treatment for the disorder.[13] Why? Milder phases of mania can seem like high-energy behavior that falls within the realm of normalcy. It can be hard

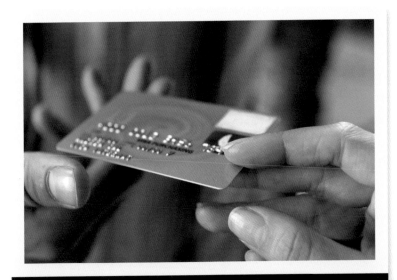

Out-of-control spending is one symptom of mania associated with bipolar disorder.

to differentiate: Is someone having an "incredibly productive" or "high energy" period in his life—or is he exhibiting the whirlwind sleeplessness of a manic phase? Is she "dating a lot" or is she becoming sexually promiscuous, another sign of mania? Has she been "going on a few shopping sprees" or is she spending money out of control and without regard to her finances? What is manic and what is normal can be a matter of a few degrees of intensity.

THE BIPOLAR HIGH

Another difficulty in diagnosing bipolar moods is how these moods feel to the person experiencing them. The depressive phase can be incredibly painful, but the manic or hypomanic phase can be pleasurable and yield tremendously productive periods of creative work. As a result, the person who is bipolar might not necessarily want this phase to end. In fact, he or she may even fear that a leveling out of moods will extinguish creative output.[14]

Episodes of both the depression and the mania of bipolar illness can emerge in varying degrees. In the manic or "high" state, people feel everything from bursts of great happiness to irritability. They often need less sleep and have a falsely increased sense of their own abilities and importance, a "king of the world" feeling. Their thoughts may race or jump from one idea to another. Doctors trying to find out if someone is having a true episode of mania often ask questions such as:

- Were you so easily distracted by things around you that you had trouble concentrating or staying on track?
- Have you been feeling so good or so hyper that other people thought you were not your normal self or were you so hyper that you got into trouble?
- Have you been much more social or outgoing than usual, for example, calling friends to talk in the middle of the night?
- Are you much more interested in sex than usual?
- Did you do things that were unusual for you or that other people might have thought were excessive, foolish, or risky?[15]

DEPRESSION AND SEXUAL BEHAVIOR AMONG U.S. MIDDLE AND HIGH SCHOOL STUDENTS

Researchers have now established a link between depression and risky sexual behaviors in middle and high school students. Risky sexual behaviors for both boys and girls included failure to use condoms or any form of birth control while having sex, abuse of a substance at the time of sex, or having multiple sexual partners. Although sexually transmitted diseases (STDs), including HIV, are often reported in the news and are important public health problems faced by adolescents, teens don't always take the proper precautions to prevent acquiring these diseases. Doctors now know that depressed teens are at an even greater risk of acquiring STDs than other teens. Researchers currently recommend that teens receive more education about depression because it affects so many important areas of their lives. Information can come in the form of screenings by family doctors, the expansion of programs for mental health education in schools, and the early identification and treatment of depression.

Researchers have discovered that depressed teens engage in more risky sexual behavior than other teens.

The link between teen girls, cervical cancer, and the human papilloma virus (HPV) makes the correlation between depression and sexual promiscuity even more compelling. HPV is a sexually transmitted infection that is extremely common among sexually active people and very hard to detect because there are no symptoms. Girls are especially vulnerable, because HPV can have a very serious health effect for women. Some types of HPV infection are associated with the development of cervical cancer. Untreated depression can be associated with promiscuity, which in turn can lead to contracting HPV and possibly cervical cancer. As a public health issue, depression ranks high among teens in many ways.[16]

BIPOLAR OR HEALTHY?

One way to understand bipolar disorder is by assessing the intensity and suddenness of the change in normal energy levels and routines that it causes. All healthy adults eat, sleep, have sex, and interact socially with others. In bipolar adults, these natural biological drives are alternately revved up or slowed down during periods of mania and depression. The fluctuations are outside their control. But doesn't everyone go through phases during which they feel more enthusiasm or periods of doldrums? Yes. For people with bipolar disorder though, these

Sleep disturbances like insomnia are a key symptom of bipolar disorder.

phases last longer, are more intense, and can disrupt their lives and the lives of those around them. Their mood swings can lead to decreases in work productivity, trouble with the law, and other major disruptions. Sometimes these phases also lead to hospitalization.

BIPOLAR DISORDER OR UNIPOLAR DEPRESSION?

Sometimes bipolar disorder first emerges not as mania but seemingly as a unipolar depression, meaning a depression without the cycles of high and low. Danger can result if a doctor does not recognize that someone who appears to have depression might actually have a more complex problem. A person with bipolar disorder who is given antidepressant medication may be inadvertently launched into a state of mania. Doctors must try to discern whether a patient who *appears* to have a unipolar depression in fact does. One important piece of information is whether or not the person has had any past behavioral problems and whether there might have been episodes of mania that were not properly diagnosed at the time. Another is whether there is a family history of bipolar disorder.[17] Finally, sleep disturbances are a key symptom of bipolar disorder and often determine whether a diagnosis will be that of bipolar disorder.

VARIATIONS ON BIPOLAR DISORDER

Just as there are different types of depression, there are also variations on the form and frequency of bipolar disorder. Episodes of either depression or mania can last from days to months. Some people do not experience depression and mania alternatively but rather feel a "mixed state" of depression with agitation. Mania can start with the feeling like that of having had too much coffee or cola: a wired-up sensation. It can end in a state of full-blown psychosis in which the person has lost touch with reality and experiences hallucinations. Another variation on bipolar disorder is rapid cycling. Sometimes individuals may experience an increased frequency of episodes. When four or more episodes of illness occur within a twelve-month period, the individual is said to have bipolar disorder with rapid cycling. Rapid cycling is more common in women.[18]

THE RISK OF SUICIDE

People with bipolar disorder are about fifteen times more likely than the general population to commit suicide. Up to 50 percent of people with bipolar disorder attempt suicide at least once in their lives and 15 percent of those with the condition die from suicide.[19] What makes someone with bipolar disorder so vulnerable to suicide? According to professor of psychiatry Kay Redfield Jamison, "Profound melancholia is . . . a pitiless, unrelenting pain that affords no window of hope . . . no respite from the horribly restless nights of despair."[20] People with major depression seek escape and relief from suffering. Yet, bipolar disorder is associated not only with the lows of depression but also with an elevation of impulsivity (or impulsiveness) that makes people act in rash and even violent ways.

Taken together, the impulsivity and the yearning to end despair can have tragic consequences. Other risk factors associated with suicide include being male, withdrawing from others, gender identity issues, having access to a gun, and having a family history of suicide.

People with bipolar disorder are about fifteen times more likely than the general population to commit suicide.

SEEKING EVALUATION AND TREATMENT

Given that depression and bipolar disorder can be life-threatening if left untreated, finding professional help is a must. But how? First, seeking out a licensed mental health professional is highly recommended. There are four major types of clinicians who treat people with mental health problems:

- **Psychiatrists** are physicians who have graduated from medical school and have specialized in the field of psychiatry, completing at least four years of specialized training called a residency. They're licensed to practice medicine in the state they work in and they also are certified by the American Board of Psychiatry and Neurology.
- **Psychologists** are graduates of doctoral programs who specialize in either research or in clinical psychology (meaning that they are licensed to treat patients). Most clinical psychologists have a PhD. Psychologists administer tests and diagnose and treat depression, but they cannot prescribe medication like medical doctors can.

- **Psychiatric nurses** are registered nurses (RNs) with master's degrees who are certified and licensed to care for psychiatric patients. Some psychiatric nurses are nurse practitioners, with an advanced nursing certificate that allows these clinical professionals to prescribe medication under supervision of a physician.
- **Social workers** are graduates of master's degree programs with a specialty in treating people with psychiatric problems and helping to integrate them back into family life and into the community.

Often a psychiatrist will work in tandem with a psychologist, psychiatric nurse, or social worker to create a regimen of therapy and medication for a patient.

RESOURCES FOR FINDING PSYCHIATRISTS

Medical centers, whether major research hospitals or community hospitals, are a good starting place for finding psychiatric help. Most medical centers have a Web site that lists staff psychiatrists. As in any other medical specialty, however, the field of psychiatry has many subspecialties, and not all doctors are equally adept at treating the same types of patients. Some specialize in children and others in adults. Another resource is the state or county chapter of the American Psychiatric Association, which lists members by region, hospital affiliation(s) and areas of specialty. Primary care physicians (family doctors) can also give referrals to psychiatrists.

The First Visit

During the first visit to a medical center or specialist's office, the doctor should spend an hour or so with the patient and his or her family going over recent history and family medical and

A Brush With Suicide

Dylan[21] was a sophomore at a top high school. Teachers always described Dylan as creative and an out-of-the-box thinker with a broad range of interests. His passions included parasailing, Russian history, and chess. Always quiet, Dylan's solitary nature intensified during his second year in high school. He spent much of his time alone in his room. His parents did not seem to notice the change. He abandoned schoolwork and created his own "curriculum" of Russian novels and plays, reading far into the night and writing long and rambling papers about the books. Still, his parents failed to notice any difference in his behavior until they returned early from a weekend away and found Dylan sitting in a car in their garage. The garage doors were closed and the car was idling. Dylan admitted that he'd been thinking of suicide. His parents rushed him to the emergency room at the nearest medical center. The psychiatrist on call examined Dylan, who admitted that he'd been planning on taking his own life for months. The doctor then admitted Dylan to the hospital for an observation period of twenty-four hours. Dylan began taking antidepressant medication and was put into an intensive outpatient program created especially for teens suffering from suicidal depression. He attended the program from 9 A.M. to 5 P.M. daily, participating in group therapy and other activities. In the groups, he made two friends who also had been struggling with depression. After two months in the program, Dylan was able to return to school full time. He worked with teachers, guidance counselors, and school administrators to make up the lost months of work. Many of the adults in Dylan's school wrote him notes while he was away. "Every day, we're grateful that you're safe and look forward to seeing you again soon," his history teacher wrote. "Most of all, we admire your bravery in making it through this dark passage and coming out whole on the other side."

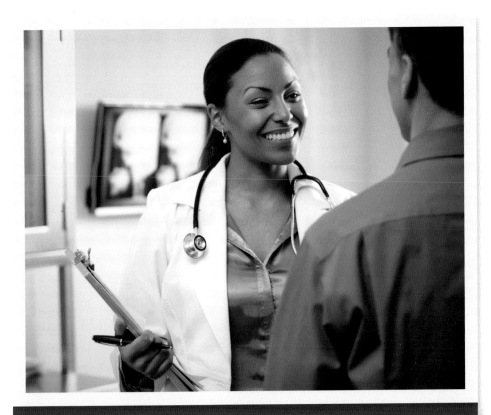

During a patient's first visit for a psychiatric evaluation, the doctor will take a number of histories, discussing any previous mental and physical illnesses, accidents, and drug or alcohol use.

psychiatric history. The doctor may evaluate a family tree and ask the patient to identify how many immediate and extended family members suffer from some form of depression, alcoholism, or drug addiction, since the three are related. The doctor will also want to know if the patient currently uses any recreational drugs, such as marijuana, meth, cocaine, or speed. This is important because the drugs can create the high experienced naturally in the manic phase. The psychiatrist will want to distinguish between a chemically produced high and one that the brain is creating on its own.

At this point, unless a patient is dangerous to himself or to others, the doctor will probably want to watch the patient closely over a period of a few weeks to see what changes occur in mood. It's very helpful for doctors to see a meticulous log of moods with dates, activities, and emotions, so they can try to track a pattern of unipolar or bipolar depression.

DIAGNOSING TEENS

Recent surveys show an alarming increase in depression among teens; in fact, as many as one in every five teens suffers from major depression.[22] Depression can be difficult to diagnose in teens because the model of depression that most doctors learn about in training is based on adult behavior. In addition, one of the cultural stereotypes about teens is that they are moody and not communicative. Teens may not be as self-aware as adults in identifying their moods, so it can be harder for the adults around them to figure out what is bothering them. Some signs of depression in teens include:

- Lack of interest in social activities
- Drop in grades
- Irritability and angry outbursts
- Drug and alcohol abuse
- Change in eating and sleeping patterns
- Changes in school performance

When teens have their first visit to a psychiatrist, it is helpful if parents bring along some documentation of their child's mood problems. This might include records from the school, a letter(s) from teachers or a guidance counselor, any police reports, and a log that the parent has kept about the teen's outward signs of emotional change. The more concrete evidence that clinicians can see during the first visit, the easier it will be for them to make an accurate diagnosis. A parent should expect that the doctor will speak with the teen alone for at least part of the appointment.

Recent surveys show an alarming increase in depression among teens.

RESPONSES OF FAMILY MEMBERS

Whether adults or teens need help, they will be met with varying responses from those closest to them, depending on the family's attitude toward emotional issues. Some family members need to be convinced that a husband, wife, son, or daughter really needs the help of a psychiatrist. They see problems with mood not as biologically based disorders but as a form of personal weakness and sometimes assign blame. It's likely that if one family member is suffering from major depression, he or she isn't alone, since the condition is often genetic. It is very important for the family to educate themselves about available resources and to work as a unit to get help as quickly as possible. Once most families realize that depression isn't "moping" but is potentially life threatening, they tend to act quickly.[23]

RESISTANCE TO TREATMENT

Often it is not the family but the depressed person who is resistant to seeking treatment. There is still a social stigma in our society about depression, particularly bipolar depression. Doctors recommend that instead of saying, "I think you seem depressed" to someone suffering from depression, the family should describe the changes in behavior they see: "I don't see you getting up to run in the morning like you used to. You seem exhausted all the time." Offer to find a psychiatrist for a loved one and to accompany him or her to the first visit. The task of seeking help might seem overwhelming to the depressed person. If resistance continues despite repeated expressions of concern, the family member might want to contact a psychiatrist ahead of time and make a preliminary visit to explain what some of the issues are. No matter how much resistance he or she finds, a family member should stick with it until the depressed person is safely in treatment. Depression generally does not "go away" by itself.[24]

It is very important for the family to educate themselves about available resources and to work as a unit to get help as quickly as possible.

HOSPITALIZATION

Like any biologically based problem, depression can be brought under control more quickly if it is caught early. Unfortunately, many people suffer with untreated or misdiagnosed depression or bipolar disorder for years. In some situations, the condition becomes so severe or dangerous that hospitalization is required. Problems ranging from denial about having a psychiatric condition, drug or alcohol abuse, and refusal to comply with a medication regimen can all lead to hospitalization. Most hospitals have a behavioral health unit, which includes a mix of patients with varying psychiatric disorders. Some also have specialized units for patients with particular psychiatric problems, such as eating disorders. Inpatient units give a patient structure, intensive therapy, and round-the-clock observation, which are especially important while necessary medication levels are being determined and when patient safety is an issue. Inpatient hospital stays are the most expensive form of treatment for mental health problems, and the immediate goal is to stabilize a patient and then bring him into a day program.[25]

Until a person can function well in daily routines, a psychiatrist might recommend that he or she attend a day program at a behavioral health center in a hospital. This is also known as a partial hospitalization program. Day programs offer individual and group therapy sessions as well as activities such as art therapy. They might also include some sort of career counseling and job placement if the patient has been out of work. Day programs are a safe harbor for people getting used to new medications. They promote positive relationships between patients and offer the support of mental health professionals on a daily basis at a critical time in a person's recovery.

Day programs can be costly, and insurance companies differ widely in what they will pay, which often falls short of the total. People with bipolar disorder frequently suffer the most from lack of insurance because the condition emerges when they are in their early to mid-twenties, when they are too old to be on their parents' health insurance plan and too young to have much savings or even health insurance of their own.

Whether hospitalization is a twenty-four-hour emergency observation, a longer in-patient stay, or an outpatient program, it's important for family members to ensure quality care. Each day, a member of the family should check in with the psychiatrist or head nurse to inquire about the patient's progress. Family members should be visible and should never hesitate to ask questions about medication or other aspects of care. People who have deteriorated to the point that they require hospitalization are in a vulnerable state. They need to rely on members of their family and their friends to advocate for them during this time of recovery.

HOW REAL PEOPLE DEAL: THE STRUGGLE OF BRITNEY SPEARS

After several months of being in the headlines for erratic behavior, Britney Spears began receiving treatment for bipolar disorder at UCLA Medical Center in February 2008. Like many people with bipolar disorder, her treatment consists of a regimen of medication paired with the support of therapy. Spears is lucky to live close to a major medical center in Los Angeles, where experienced psychiatrists and researchers can draw on their knowledge of bipolar disorder to help her. She sees physicians regularly, and they are just a phone call away whenever she needs them. With her symptoms under control, Spears regained the right to visitation with her sons. She also began working once again, performing in some guest roles on television. In the singer's case, her parents intervened to get her the medical care that she needed. Although her life has been chaotic, Spears is fortunate in that she has family support and the financial resources she needs to get her career and relationship with her children back on track.[26]

Britney Spears's struggle with bipolar disorder was widely covered by the news media.

Treatment of Depression and Bipolar Disorder

L ike any physical illness, mood disorders require prompt attention. The first line of treatment for depression is talk therapy with a trained professional. The therapist—a psychiatrist, psychologist, psychiatric nurse, or clinical social worker—will help identify the type and severity of the depression and will work with a patient to set goals for recovery.

Talk therapy is useful in many ways. It carves out time when an individual can intensely focus on thoughts and feelings with the guidance of a skilled and impartial listener. Some goals of talk therapy are to

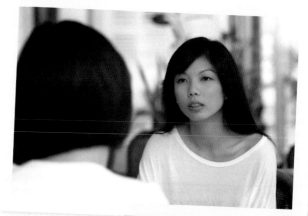

Talk therapy is the first line of treatment for depression.

- Understand a mood disorder
- Overcome fears or insecurities
- Cope with stress
- Make sense of past traumatic experiences
- Separate a true personality from the mood swings caused by illness
- Identify triggers that worsen symptoms
- Improve relationships with friends and family
- Establish a stable, dependable routine
- Develop a plan for coping with crisis

- End destructive habits, such as drinking, using drugs, and risky sex
- Address symptoms such as changes in eating or sleeping habits or increased levels of anxiety, anger, or irritability
- Develop a relationship with a trusted resource[1]

TYPES OF TALK THERAPY

There are many types of talk therapy, and the practice has evolved with increased understanding of mood and human emotions. When psychotherapy was first practiced by Freud, patients committed years to the process. It was time-consuming and very expensive, so beneficiaries of the practice were largely limited to the upper classes. Today, talk therapies are short-term and targeted, with the aim of helping people achieve independent and productive lives as efficiently as possible. Two of the most popular forms of goal-oriented therapy are cognitive behavior therapy and interpersonal therapy.[2]

Cognitive Behavior Therapy

Cognitive behavior therapy is based on the view that pessimistic thoughts can significantly contribute to depression. Negative thinking is a pattern that can be broken if depressed people can step away from their pessimistic perspective, according to cognitive therapists. Negative thought patterns include the following:

- Catastrophizing—Expecting the worst to happen at all times. "I've been feeling tired lately so I must be depressed!"
- Overgeneralizing—Seeing one small misstep as the beginning of a downfall. "I hit two foul balls during practice today. I'm never going to play baseball well."

- Personalizing—Thinking that everything is your own fault or goes awry because of something you did wrong. "My boss is very quiet today. I wonder if he's mad at me."
- All-or-nothing thinking—Either people or things are great or they are a disaster, with no middle ground. "If I can't get straight A's, then I'm never going to get into a good college, so my life will be a failure."
- Emotionalizing—Allowing emotions to cloud judgment. "If I'm not invited to this party, it means that no one wants to be around me."
- Filtering—Hearing only the negatives and not the positives in a conversation. "I got the silver medal in the arts show. I'm second rate."

ASHLEY, A NEGATIVE THINKER

Ashley[3] was working her way through college and took a summer job at an exclusive clothing boutique for women. She made a low salary but earned a generous commission for sales. On her second day, the boutique's owner asked to speak with her, and Ashley panicked. "I'm going to get fired," she thought. In fact, the owner wanted to know if Ashley would like to join the sales team for a special after-work barbeque at the end of the week. Next, Ashley helped a woman and her daughter, who tried on several outfits but left the boutique empty-handed. "I'm horrible at this," Ashley thought. "I'm never going to make any money." She wondered how she'd be able to pay for her books the following semester and confided to a co-worker, "I've been here three days and I can see what's

Continued on next page

Continued from previous page

going to happen. I'm not stylish enough myself to sell these clothes, and no one will want to buy them from me." Ashley left the boutique nearly in tears at the end of her shift, convinced that she was a failure and that accepting the job had been a disastrous mistake. It was the end of her third day at a new job.

Ashley's negative assumptions about her job performance were all unhealthy and inaccurate. She anticipated the worst when her boss asked to speak with her; she saw a mildly troubling event, missing a big sale, as the start of an unending cycle; she interpreted missing the sale as a personal reflection on her abilities; and she allowed her feelings about what was going on to cloud her judgment.

A person with a more positive pattern of thoughts might have experienced exactly what Ashley did and concluded that her boss must really like her to take the time to speak with her and include her in the barbeque; that the lost sale was no big deal because she was just learning the new job; and that next time she'd get an even bigger commission using her new experience at selling clothing. Cognitive therapists believe that positive thinkers will find more success and happiness in life because they expect it, but negative thinkers are vulnerable to depression because they anticipate the worst.

Cognitive behavior therapists work with patients to break old thought patterns and replace them with more realistic ones. It is a short-term and goal-oriented therapy that requires willing participation by the patient. Cognitive behavior therapy can also be used with people who are suffering from both milder and major depression.

Interpersonal Therapy and Other Therapies

Interpersonal therapy is another popular talk therapy technique. It brings to light old conflicts about key occurrences in the patient's life, such as those involving loss or grief, transitions, and conflict. It gives people tools to work through troubled relationships or events that may cause or deepen depression. Interpersonal therapy, like cognitive therapy, usually lasts from twelve to twenty sessions[4] and is designed to give a patient a hand during a particularly stressful time in his or her life.

Other talk therapies include group therapy, couples therapy, and family therapy. The therapeutic process gives patients a safe outlet for expressing feelings. It aims to change negative thoughts and behavior patterns. For those diagnosed with major depression, therapy can provide a crucial support in monitoring their moods while medication is being adjusted. It can also be a relief to patients to know that in times of mood change, which can make anyone feel out of control, they can depend on a reliable professional to help them cope. This is

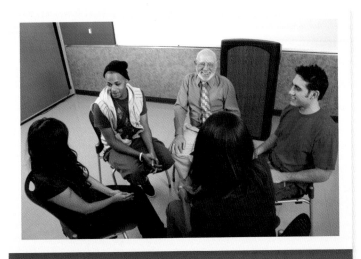

Group therapy is a helpful form of talk therapy.

one of the reasons why it's important for someone who has been diagnosed with major depression to complete a course of therapy.

REBALANCING BRAIN CHEMISTRY WITH MEDICATION

For people with mild to moderate depression, talk therapy alone can facilitate recovery, but those with more serious depression or with bipolar disorder require medication in addition to therapy. For these people, a skilled psychiatrist is an indispensable part of the treatment team. Matching mood disorders to medications is a sophisticated science, especially at a time when an increasing number of medications are available for the treatment of depression. The category of medications used to treat mood disorders is known as psychotropic drugs.

Matching mood disorders to medications is a sophisticated science.

Psychotropic Drugs

In the 1960s, there were many major milestones in the discovery and development of psychotropic drugs and the understanding of how they work in the brain. During this era, scientists also honed their knowledge of neurotransmitters, chemical messengers between nerve cells in the brain. They established the relationship between insufficient levels of neurotransmitters, and depression and were able to name some of the principal neurotransmitters: norepinephrine, serotonin, and dopamine.

All major psychotropic drugs, such as antidepressants and antipsychotic medications, affect the releasing and re-absorbing of neurotransmitters among neurons in the brain. Antidepressants come in three main categories:

- Tricyclic antidepressants
- Monoamine oxidase inhibitors (MAOIs)
- Selective serotonin reuptake inhibitors (SSRIs)

With all of these medicines, patients must take doses for at least three to four weeks before they benefit fully from them. Many people think that being on a psychotropic medication will give them a "high" or make them an addict. In reality, this class of medication is not addictive and simply helps the person taking it from feeling the crushing effects of major depression. As one person put it: "I thought that medication was going to make me weird or an addict. But after a few months of taking it I only feel better. There is no "high." I just feel a lot less depressed and able to cope with life. I can deal with things that used to make me cry and want to hide."[5]

Tricyclic antidepressants

Tricyclics were the first known group of antidepressants. They increase the amount of the neurotransmitters serotonin and norepinephrine in the brain, lessening depression. Tricyclics were a breakthrough in psychotropic medications, but they had many undesirable side effects, including blurred vision and weight gain. For some people with bipolar disorder, tricyclics can trigger a manic state. In addition, these drugs may pose a risk to patients with heart disease and can be fatal if overdosed intentionally. Some widely prescribed tricyclics are Elavil, Norpramin, and Tofranil.[6]

Monoamine oxidase inhibitors (MAOIs)

The MAOIs keep the level of neurotransmitters high within the brain by inhibiting (preventing) their chemical break-down. Specifically, this type of antidepressant works on the neurotransmitters epinephrine, norepinephrine, and dopamine.

Generic and Brand Name Drugs

Most products that consumers buy have brand names such as Skippy peanut butter and Nike sneakers. These names are well researched and carefully selected to give the product a particular image and appeal. The names of prescription drugs are also well researched and are created to help market the medication to both physicians and consumers. Pharmaceutical companies have big marketing budgets to create appealing names for drugs before they are launched into the marketplace. For example, the blockbuster SSRI fluoxetine is marketed as Prozac by the Eli Lilly company. When Lilly was preparing to bring fluoxetine to market in the 1970s, it hired the company Interbrand to help give the drug a catchy name that would be memorable to the public. Interbrand had a great track record creating winning brands for companies as diverse as Sony, Microsoft, and Nintendo. The name "Prozac" was chosen because it gave a positive and snappy ring to a drug that treats depression. (Think of the associations with the "pro" in the name.) Prozac was marketed as a drug free of side effects (in contrast with the earlier generation of antidepressants, the tricyclics). By the time the drug was available in pharmacies, patients knew about it and were asking physicians for it by name.

In 2000, shortly before Lilly's patent on the drug expired, Prozac had 40 million users in the United States. It was the fifth most commonly prescribed drug in the United States, and earned $3 billion in the year 2000 for its manufacturer.[7] The word "Prozac" became synonymous with SSRIs in the public mind. In August 2001, the drug was released from its patent, allowing other drug manufacturers to produce their own versions. Other generic and brand names of commonly prescribed SSRIs include:

Generic Name	Brand Name
citalopram	Celexa
fluvoxamine	Luvox
paroxetine	Paxil
sertraline	Zoloft

Though they are highly effective, MAOIs are infrequently prescribed because of their serious side effects. Many foods and medications must be avoided by people taking this drug. One of the chief side effects of the drug is a fatal rise in blood pressure if guidelines aren't followed strictly.[8]

Selective serotonin reuptake inhibitors (SSRIs)

SSRIs are the newest and most popular types of antidepressant medications because they have fewer side effects than MAOIs or tricyclic antidepressants. Developed in the 1980s, SSRIs improve mood by increasing the amount of the chemical messenger serotonin, which travels between nerve cells in the brain. Whereas tricyclic antidepressants focused on three transmitters associated with mood—serotonin, dopamine, and norepinenephrine—SSRIs concentrate on just one. SSRIs usually take three to six weeks to become fully effective and to improve depression. One of their chief benefits is that this class of antidepressants can be safely taken with most other medications. People who use SSRIs describe feeling more stable, outgoing, trusting, and less hostile.

However, SSRIs do have one unwanted side effect. Many who take SSRIs find that there are changes in sexual functioning or a loss of sex drive. In fact, research shows that between 20 and 45 percent of people experience a decline in their ability to enjoy sex when they take SSRIs. Those who find this particular aspect of SSRIs intolerable frequently chose to take the non-SSRI medication Wellbutrin, which has little or no effect on sexual function or performance.[9]

Teens and SSRIs When SSRIs were first introduced to the public, many physicians saw the drugs as an important new tool in the struggle against teen suicide. From 2002 to 2003, antidepressant prescriptions for teens rose by 36 percent. However, public awareness about the use of SSRIs in teens increased not because the medication was linked to suicide prevention, but because it was linked to actual suicide in several widely reported cases. By October 2004, the Food and Drug Administration established its strongest warning—a "black box" warning—about SSRIs. (Such warnings are called black box warnings because they are printed within strong black lines.) Since then, teen SSRI antidepressant use has dropped about 10 percent a year. There is still controversy about use of SSRIs and teens among public health experts. Many felt that the FDA was justified, but others say that the federal agency buckled unnecessarily to unfounded public opinion and that teens are the losers in this debate. Most practitioners who care for teens still consider SSRIs a critical and valuable medication responsible for saving many lives.[10]

From 2002 to 2003, antidepressant prescriptions for teens rose by 36 percent.

Finding the Right Antidepressant Medication

Since 2005, advances in medical science have produced new medications that can relieve unnecessary emotional distress and allow many people to be much more productive with an improved mood. Recurrent stresses and distress produce depression by depletion of neurotransmitter chemicals in the brain.

After a few months of stresses and distress, it is sometimes very difficult for a person to make sufficient changes on his own in order to relieve the depletion of neurotransmitters. Many people react by numbing their feelings and emotional distress with alcohol or marijuana. Others use stimulants like speed as a short-term fix, which actually further deplete the neurotransmitters. One useful mechanism to improve neuro-transmitters is very frequent exercise. Many people over fifty

A Teen With Bipolar Disorder on Medication

After two episodes of major depression followed by mania, William[11] was hospitalized at a major medical center near his home in suburban Illinois. The nineteen-year-old was stabilized on Eskalith, the brand name version of lithium, and his family was relieved and thankful for the excellent medical care he received. William left college for the semester and lived at home the following summer, expecting to earn some money doing landscaping. A high-school lacrosse player, he was tall and strong and loved physical activity. It dismayed him when he started noticing changes in his body. "I felt so sluggish," William said. "It was as though I'd lost about 40 percent of my physical coordination and energy. It took me about twice as long as the other guys on my crew to weed-whack a lawn. I also developed a noticeable tremor in my hands, which was embarrassing." But the worst thing was the thirst. "No matter how much I drank, I needed more water fifteen minutes later, so I always had to use the bathroom. It was as though I'd suddenly traded bodies with my grandfather. I hated it."

William's physician, with whom he checked in once a week, switched him from lithium to an anticonvulsant medication. "The mood stabilizer worked much better for me," William said. "It balanced out my moods without as many side effects. I did gain about ten pounds right after I went on it, but I started running every day and cutting way down on carbs, so that halted the weight gain." William returned to college in the fall and continued with a normal course of studies, minus the alcohol, which his doctor told him to avoid. "No medication is perfect," William said, "but I'm not looking for perfection, just a shot at a normal life."

years old already have relative depletion of neurotransmitters, and they usually find that appropriate medication is a great benefit.[12]

The outward signs of depression differ by age and gender. One commonly repeated saying is that "Women often get sad, but men get mad." Men show anger and frustration, and may be easily upset. Women may experience worry, fear, and little joy in life.

So, what are the downsides of such antidepressant medications? There are about a half dozen common ones that have been used with many years of clinical success. Most doctors would agree that there is nothing to lose—and everything to gain—by prescribing them and seeing which one is best for an individual. Doctor visits are required, but this necessary investment in time is more than worth the improvement in quality of life. Of the most commonly prescribed antidepressants, it is likely that only one or two would optimally benefit a person with minimal side effects. So, it is often necessary to try a few different ones before finding the one with no side effects and its best dose for the individual. It usually takes a few days to be sure side effects are absent, and a few weeks to know if the medicine helps the person. Sometimes the doctor needs to increase the dose for better results, or prescribes another antidepressant.

Most doctors would agree that the benefits of antidepressant medications vastly outweigh the downsides.

It is important that during treatment with such antidepressant medication, which may last a few months or years, the patient reports to the prescribing doctor if he or she has suicidal thoughts or more suicidal thoughts than usual. After taking such medication for a while, some patients no longer feel it's necessary to continue taking their medication. However, such patients should not simply stop taking it without first talking to their physician.

Most individuals who have found the right medicine and their best dose can expect to feel more joy in life and spend less time feeling angry, discontented, distressed, sad, and easily upset. After a few weeks they may feel more comfortable, at ease, tolerant, and may be more flexible; they might also feel easygoing and have a more positive attitude. With a brighter outlook, they can have more coping ability, overall effectiveness, and employability.

The physician may start with Prozac (fluoxetine), then try other drugs like Wellbutrin or Paxil (paroxetine). A trial of each may be given as a half dose for a few days (watching for unacceptable side effects), a full dose for a month, then if no effect, a higher dose for another month. Obviously it may take time to find the best medication and the right dose.[13, 14]

MEDICATION FOR BIPOLAR DISORDER

Just as antidepressant medications changed the lives of people suffering from major depression, the drug lithium enabled people with bipolar disorder to regain control over their moods. It was first prescribed for widespread use in the United States in the early 1970s. In fact, the ancient Roman physician Soranus of Ephesus noticed that when patients with emotional problems drank water from the alkaline springs in the area, their state of mind improved. Today, those springs, located in Italy and other places in southern Europe, are known for their lithium content.[15]

What Is SAD?

SAD is an acronym for seasonal affective disorder, a type of depression that is triggered by the shorter days of winter. While many people experience a mild form of winter blues and dislike the season's dark and cold, people with SAD respond to diminished sunlight with symptoms of major depression: weepiness, fatigue, and sleeping disorders such as insomnia.

According to the National Institutes of Health (NIH), most SAD symptoms stem from out-of-kilter circadian rhythms, the natural rhythms of the body. Because of diminished daylight, the brain is confused by the lack of sun and responds by producing hormone and neurotransmitter levels that lead to depression.

In the 1980s, doctors began treating SAD patients with light therapy, replacing natural daylight with intense artificial light. Patients use a device called a light box that is portable and small enough to fit on a table at home. The light box emits a spectrum of light that mimics natural sunlight. People sit in front of the box with their eyes open for up to two hours a day (most people sit for less than an hour). They don't stare directly at the light, but rather read, write, eat a meal, or perform another task while the light enters their eyes.[16]

Snowy days with less sunlight can trigger the brain into producing the hormone and neurotransmitter levels that cause depression.

Light therapy alleviates the symptoms of SAD in the

majority of patients. In one experiment at Columbia University in New York City, 75 percent of SAD patients improved with an average light exposure of thirty minutes a day of light therapy. The amount of time necessary to relieve depression varied from person to person. The approximately 25 percent of people who don't find relief from SAD with light therapy generally begin a course of antidepressant medication.

In 2006, researchers from the National Institute of Mental Health (NIMH) found in a study that combining a low dose of the light-sensitive hormone melatonin in the afternoon in addition to bright light in the morning helped speed improvement and stabilize SAD patients.[17]

Lithium

Lithium is effective at controlling mood swings in all types of bipolar disorder (Bipolar I, Bipolar II, rapid cycling), and has proven effective in 60 to 70 percent of the people who take it. People who take lithium must get regular blood tests. If it is too concentrated in the blood, lithium can become toxic and even deadly—and if the dose isn't high enough, it is ineffective.

Lithium begins to ease the symptoms of bipolar disorder about a week after people first take it. Because it flushes easily out of the body with urination, it must be taken regularly, generally several times a day. No one knows exactly why this naturally occurring element is so effective at controlling cycles of mania and depression. Most people with bipolar disorder tolerate prescription lithium's potential side effects well. These can include thirst, weight gain, some muscular tremors, and feeling "in a fog."

Are Alcoholism and Depression Related?

When someone has a drinking problem, is the trouble primarily with alcohol or with mood? Any psychological professional who is trying to help someone who has a problem with drinking should first determine whether or not an underlying depression is coming into play. It often is. Doctors now place alcoholism in the category of mood disorders that includes depression.[18]

In fact, mania, depression, suicidal tendencies, and alcoholism all run concurrently through families. This is why a thorough family history is so important in accurately diagnosing a person. Scientists have noted and explored the possibility of a common genetic trait that ties together these mood disorders and an inability to manage stress. Some have focused on chromosome 11 as a point of research.[19]

Knowing that this link exists, even if it is not fully understood, has led to the use of SSRIs to help alcoholics stop drinking and stay sober. As more is learned about the connection between emotional problems such as alcoholism and depression that were once seen as unrelated, an increasing number of people may be able to lead sober lives.

Disorders such as depression and alcoholism are often found in members of the same family.

Anticonvulsant Medications

Those people with bipolar disorder who find that the side effects of litium outweigh its benefits are often prescribed various forms of valproic acid for relief of their symptoms. Valproate, also known as valproic acid, is an anticonvulsant medication that was originally used to treat seizure disorders such as epilepsy.[20] Valproic acid, known in its most popular commercial form as Depakote, has also come into use as a mood stabilizer. Side effects of valproic acid can include hair thinning and significant weight gain. This medication can also irritate the liver, a more dangerous consequence of its use. Depakote levels in the blood must be regularly monitored, as with lithium, so people who take it should have regular blood tests.[21] Newer types of anticonvulsant medications include lamotrigine, sold as Lamictal, and topiramate, sold as Topamax.

During an episode of psychosis people who are delusional might imagine that they have great creative powers and will become a rock star or a famous painter.

Another frequently prescribed mood stabilizer for bipolar disorder is a class of drug called carbamazepine and manufactured by pharmaceutical companies as Tegretol, Carbatrol, or Atretol.[22] Regarded chiefly as backup medications for those who can't tolerate either lithium or valproic acid, these medications can bring unwanted side effects, specifically nausea and mild problems with memory.[23]

Antipsychotics

During the manic phase of bipolar disorder, people can experience profoundly disordered thinking, such as delusions or hallucinations. This type of skewed thinking is called psychosis. During an episode of psychosis people who are delusional might imagine that they have great creative powers and will become a rock star or a famous painter. People with hallucinations see or hear things that aren't really present. A group of medications called antipsychotics brings this thinking under control. Clozaril (marketed as Clozapine), risperidone (sold as Risperdal) and Olanzapine (brand name Zyprexa) are all antipsychotic medications that are currently in use.[24] Doctors generally prescribe this class of drugs as a temporary measure to calm a patient enough to create a treatment plan. Unlike lithium or anticonvulsant medications, the antipsychotics are generally not part of a lifetime care regimen.

Electroconvulsive Therapy: If All Else Fails

What happens when patients with depression or bipolar disorder don't respond to medication? If people are at the point of being suicidal or hospitalized because medication fails to control their depression, physicians may recommend a course of electroconvulsive therapy (ECT) sessions. Patients receiving ECT are administered general anesthesia to relax their muscles and prevent a full seizure. A physician then uses an ECT machine to artificially produce a seizure in the brain, sparking the production of neurotransmitters and moderating mood. Because ECT was often overused and misused when it was first introduced in the 1950s, many people still consider it barbaric. But modern use of ECT is much safer and more targeted because the medical devices used to implement it have been refined and deliver a much milder electrical charge. While the procedure does cause some temporary loss of short-term memory, it can also save lives.

CIRCADIAN RHYTHMS

Once medication or other therapy has stabilized mood, it's important to establish a regular schedule of sleeping and waking to help regulate the natural rhythms of the body, called the circadian rhythms. As daytime (diurnal) creatures, humans have evolved to be awake and active during the day and asleep at night when it is dark out. Reversing that pattern can sometimes produce the symptoms of depression even if people have no history of family depression.

Circadian rhythms are established by a "clock" in the brain. Every morning when people wake up, light enters their eyes. The light sends a signal to the brain, letting the brain know where it is in a twenty-four-hour day. That first cue of light is essential for establishing the proper timing of melatonin hormone release in the human body.

Waking up and exposing oneself to daylight also sets a "clock" in the body that gives people a full day's worth of mental alertness and energy. As light fades, people begin to slow down until at night, about sixteen hours after they first awoke, people's brains begin to produce the hormones, such as melatonin, that lull them to sleep. They sleep for a consolidated period of about eight hours, and the process begins again in the morning.

When circadian rhythms are shifted, people don't function as well. One example of this is jet lag. Flying from one time zone into another causes loss of sleep and, more critically, it confuses the brain. Suddenly, day is moved forward or back three to twelve hours, disturbing circadian rhythms and the hormone release cycle. People with jet lag often feel exhausted, irritable, and even a bit depressed—all responses to shifting circadian rhythms. Since fluctuating sleep patterns are associated with bipolar disorder, it's important for patients with bipolar disorder to stick to a regular sleep-wake schedule and for their daylight hours to be active ones that include exercise and nutritious food.[25]

SOCIAL RHYTHM THERAPY

Interpersonal and Social Rhythm Therapy (IPSRT) is a treatment program that stresses maintaining a regular schedule of daily activities and stability in personal relationships as an effective therapy for bipolar disorder. One study conducted by researchers at the University of Pittsburgh School of Medicine found that IPSRT helped prevent symptoms over a two-year period.

Jet lag is an example of people not functioning well when circadian rhythms are shifted.

Therapists who use IPSRT recommend it because they've found that disruptions in daily routines and problems in interpersonal relationships can trigger manic and depressive episodes in people with bipolar disorder. During the treatment, therapists help patients understand how changes in daily routines and the quality of their relationships with friends and family can sometimes worsen or improve their symptoms. Awareness of the stress that certain situations can bring helps people manage their relationships better.

"Our study shows that this form of psychotherapy is helpful to many people with bipolar disorder," said Ellen Frank, PhD, professor of psychiatry at the University of Pittsburgh School of Medicine and Western Psychiatric Institute and Clinic, and principal investigator of the study. "Second, it shows that the type of psychotherapy we choose for a patient should depend on the individual's circumstances. Treatment for bipolar is not 'one-size-fits-all.' We have shown that IPSRT is a powerful tool in the prevention of illness recurrence."[26]

Together with talk therapy, SSRIs and exercise are the mainstay of treatment.

EXERCISE AND MOOD

One way to help sleep and improve mood is to exercise daily. People who exercise have more consolidated sleep, meaning that they experience fewer awakenings throughout the night. Aerobic exercise, which gets the heart beating quickly, triggers the release of hormones called endorphins that make people feel good and lift their mood. Exercise such as running, brisk walking, biking, playing basketball, dancing, or swimming all boost mood by releasing not only endorphins but also the neurotransmitters serotonin and norepinephrine. One study in Canada demonstrated that aerobic exercise three to five times a week was as effective as an SSRI medication. Together with talk therapy, SSRIs and exercise are the mainstay of treatment. A good combination of activities is an aerobic exercise followed by a few minutes of yoga, stretching, or gentle breathing so that the body can fully relax and benefit from the activity.[27]

FOOD AND MOOD

For several decades, researchers have been exploring connections between what people eat and their state of mind. Eating a variety of nutritious foods, such as whole grains, low-fat dairy products, fresh fruits, and leafy green vegetables is beneficial for anyone, but especially for people facing the challenges of a mood disorder.

People with major depression often struggle with unwanted weight loss, especially if anxiety accompanies the depression. The loss of appetite can take a toll on energy and cause enough of a weight drop to make someone appear ill or frail. Nutritionists recommend eating protein to rebuild cells and gain strength while also increasing fat content. For someone dropping body fat, leafy green vegetables and fresh fruits should be supplemented with high-fat foods such as cheeseburgers and fries.[28]

One nutrient that is especially important is vitamin C. Investigators in India gave people with the brain disease schizophrenia large amounts of vitamin C. These researchers found significant improvement in the mood of the patients. They also found success with vitamin E and omega-3 fatty acids, found in coldwater fish. Other scientists have recreated their findings, especially those involving omega-3 fatty acids.[29]

Vitamin supplements and healthy eating are not a substitute for medications. They lay the groundwork for overall health, which improves mood and quality of life for anyone. As important as healthy eating is the elimination of drugs that can complicate mood disorders. Replacing caffeine and alcohol with healthier drinks, such as fruit juice or water is a good place to begin. Alcohol contains many calories and no nutrients; moreover, it is a mood depressant, and anyone on psychotropic medication should consult with a doctor before using any alcohol—even in small quantities. Because anticonvulsant medications often cause weight gain, people taking them should make an extra effort to exercise and eat a low-fat, high-fiber diet.

Living With Depression and Bipolar Disorder

After an episode of depression or mania has passed and people are stabilized on medication, they find themselves not at the end but at the beginning of a long road. Managing major depression or bipolar disorder is a lifetime commitment. Once someone has been properly diagnosed and treated, the mood disorder does not vanish. People with depression and bipolar disorder are particularly vulnerable in the first months after diagnosis, when they are getting used to new medications and adjusting to a different lifestyle, and that vulnerability includes increased risk of suicide.

Exercise is an important part of maintaining a successful recovery from a mood disorder.

So, what is necessary to turn the corner and live a healthy and balanced life, even in the face of a lifetime mood disorder? Studies show that people who can accept their genetic blueprint and do all they can to take care of themselves do the best. The most successful make lifestyle changes to minimize the impact of their condition. These adjustments include taking medication faithfully, maintaining contact with a therapist, sticking to a regular schedule, paying attention to diet and exercise, and being vigilant about keeping stress to a minimum. Many make the mistake of going off their medicines when they feel "better."[1]

A Bipolar Detour From Paris to Columbia

Lizzie Simon, a teen with bipolar disorder, wrote *Detour*, a memoir about the shattering of her "perfect life" and her recovery. She traces her first awareness of bipolar disorder to her senior year of high school and the day she found out she was accepted to Columbia University. A native of Rhode Island, Lizzie was living with friends of her family in Paris and attending an international school when the bipolar symptoms first appeared. "I remember a little fuzz building in my head," she writes. "I remember the plane ride home for Christmas and getting very drunk in the last row with a guy who looked like Kurt Cobain." After that, depression set in. She cried continually and then went to see a psychiatrist, who prescribed the antidepressant Paxil. A few weeks later, back in Paris, she was at a friend's house and found herself in a psychotic state that produced terrifying hallucinations. Her friends helped her seek treatment at a hospital in Paris, where one of the doctors told her that she probably had bipolar disorder and not depression. She stopped taking antidepressant medication immediately, flew home, and consulted a psychiatrist. On the advice of her new doctor, she began taking lithium. It worked. "Lithium gave me a functional brain," she writes. She went on to have a successful freshman year at Columbia but longed to meet other people her age that had gone through a similar experience. She criss-crossed America in search of them and wrote about her experience in *Detour*. Lizzie continues to take her lithium and do well.[2]

Organizing medications in medication containers labeled with days of the week helps patients with bipolar disorder stick to their routines.

THE MOOD CHART

Self-awareness is one important part of maintaining a healthy mood. A mood chart is an indispensable tool for keeping track of the highs and lows of daily energy levels and feelings. It also encourages reflection on mood, turning the thought, *Life is exhausting, and I'll never keep up* into *I can see that my mood is down today and so is my energy. That's why I'm having negative thoughts.*

A useful mood chart will include a place to check off medications taken, a section to record hours of sleep each night, and an area where significant or stressful events can be briefly noted (i.e., "Argument with friend today"). The largest section of the chart, however, should include a place to make daily notations about mood—specifically, mania, depression, and anxiety—and to describe the intensity of each mood, from mild to severe. In a well-maintained mood chart, patterns of mood quickly emerge. For example, if it becomes clear that a female patient's moods are shifting during her menstrual cycles, a physician will want to know that information to be able to evaluate how well her medication is working.[3]

THE IMPORTANCE OF ROUTINES

When people's moods shift continually, it's often hard to establish routines, so people with depression and bipolar disorder, especially the latter, frequently lack consistency in their lives. Routines benefit all people, but especially those with depression, for several reasons: They create a sense of external order and stability, they enable greater productivity, and they're energy savers. If people establish a routine for taking their medication (for example, placing daily doses in a special medication container, labeled with the days of the week), they increase the likelihood of actually taking their pills.

Routines benefit all people, but especially those with depression.

Routines can be a challenge. They go against the grain of a life with bipolar disorder, which is characterized by shifts and swings of high energy, spontaneity, and manic sociability followed by a period of sluggish inactivity. People with bipolar disorder can perceive routines as boring after the drama of manic highs and crashes. Nevertheless, people with bipolar disorder can benefit from routines perhaps more than any other group because, as mood shifts, routine can bring order to lives that would otherwise feel out of control. Helpful routines might include:

- Eating dinner with family, or at least having one weekend family dinner when everyone can get together.
- Taking a walk every day, either in the morning or at night.

- Reading every night before bed (and perhaps having a subscription to a favorite magazine with which to relax).
- Packing a lunch for work or school to boost nutrition and eliminate excess calories.
- Choosing all outfits for the week on a Sunday and making sure your clothing is clean and ready to go in order to make mornings—the most difficult time of day for people with depression—more manageable.[4]

SLEEP

Sleep problems are one of the symptoms of depression and bipolar disorder. Sleep and mood are intertwined, and people who live with depression and bipolar disorder experience irregular sleep patterns and disturbed circadian rhythms. Insomnia, especially, is very common among depressed patients, but so is hypersomnia, which is oversleeping. According to the National Sleep Foundation, not only do people with depression experience insomnia, but people who don't get the correct amount of high-quality sleep in the right timeframe can become depressed; in fact, they run a ten-fold risk of doing so.[5]

Sleep and mood are intertwined, and good sleep habits can help ensure a restful night's sleep.

Many people with chronic depression know well the feeling of lying in bed, waiting to fall asleep (sleep onset insomnia). Many also know firsthand the frustration of the most common sleep disturbance that accompanies depression, "early morning waking" (sleep maintenance insomnia). Typically, people with this problem fall asleep but find themselves suddenly awake at about 3:00 A.M., often feeling anxious.

Good sleep habits can help ensure a restful night's sleep.

Many psychiatrists hesitate to add prescription sleep aids to the mix of medications that their patients with depression or bipolar disorder are already taking. However, people need not rely on sleeping pills. Good sleep habits can help ensure a restful night's sleep. Like dental hygiene, sleep "hygiene" must be learned and practiced regularly to be beneficial, but just a few weeks' practice can yield impressive improvement. Sleep hygiene rules suggested by the National Sleep Foundation include the following:

- Create a restful sanctuary in the bedroom, saving it for sleep only. Do not bring work into the bedroom or watch TV there. Remove anything that projects artificial light, including televisions. A clock with illuminated numbers should be turned toward the wall. The most restful color for a bedroom is blue.
- Invest in a good set of curtains or blinds to totally block out all light. Humans have evolved to be in total darkness at night, so keep the bedroom free from street lights.
- Establish a restful bedtime routine. Your brain needs about an hour to wind down before bed and start releasing sleep-inducing hormones. Turn off the computer and television, which are too stimulating, sixty minutes before bed. Take a bath, read, or drink some herbal tea while listening to soothing music.
- If you can't sleep in the middle of the night, don't toss and turn in bed. Get up and sit in another room. If something is bothering you, write in a journal, ending with the words, "I will deal with this tomorrow when I'm rested."

POST-TRAUMATIC STRESS DISORDER (PTSD)

Post-traumatic stress disorder is an anxiety disorder that surfaces after a traumatic event. One of the side effects of this disorder is major depression. PTSD is common in survivors of violent acts (such as rape) or a violent environment (such as war). Approximately 8 million Americans have PTSD, including emergency responders, victims of terrorist attacks, and survivors of serious automobile crashes or domestic violence—all are susceptible to PTSD. For example, a 2004 study in *The New England Journal of Medicine* found that 15.6 to 17.1 percent of soldiers who had been deployed to Iraq and 11.2 percent of soldiers who had been deployed to Afghanistan returned home with PTSD. The study was conducted through an anonymous survey. The study also concluded that there was a "significant risk of mental health problems" and that soldiers "reported important barriers to receiving mental health services."[7]

Symptoms of PTSD can occur right after the event(s) that triggered it, or they can surface months or even years later. The symptoms of PTSD are unlikely to go away on their own, especially if they have been present for years. But many short-term therapies have been successful, including using computer reenactments to help soldiers suffering from PTSD relive their war experiences and try to make sense of them.[8] Medication can also be helpful, and SSRIs are the usual type of antidepressant prescribed.

It's important for people with PTSD to find support, but they tend to withdraw from friends and family, feeling that they are to blame for their own symptoms.[9] It's important for the people around those suffering with PTSD to encourage their loved ones to seek professional help.

Then, distract yourself with a calm activity. Reading is best because the back-and-forth movement of the eyes during reading mimics the motion of eyes during REM sleep, the stage in which dreaming occurs.

- Exercise is a fantastic aid to sleep. Exercising at least two to three hours before sleep encourages a deeper sleep with fewer awakenings.[6] Exercising vigorously too close to bedtime can prove overly stimulating and disruptive to sleep, however.

STRESS

Stress is intertwined with mood disorders in complex ways. Many of the changes in brain chemistry that can be seen in a depressed person actually are caused by an increase in the hormone cortisol, released in response to stress. In fact, recent data shows that nearly 70 percent of depressive episodes are somehow connected to a stressful experience. Researchers also know that repeated stress in childhood can predispose a person to be especially vulnerable to depression for the rest of their lives.[10]

What exactly is stress? Stress is the fight-or-flight reaction that spurs our bodies to go on hyper alert and produce adrenaline, a hormone the body produces in response to stress. Stress is a physical response that occurs because of a perceived threat. Thousands of years ago, the threat was something you could see or feel: wild animals or another tangible challenge to survival.

Today, stress is more likely to be activated by people or situations that cause feelings of anxiety, uncertainty, or insecurity. Common sources of stress include work; conflict with family members, romantic partners, or within other relationships; and thought patterns that include unreasonably

Stress is a part of life and cannot be avoided; coping with stress requires that one recognize triggers.

high expectations of oneself or perfectionism. One reason that stress is so powerful is that the body can't distinguish between what is real and what is merely perceived. Each day, as we encounter stress, the body triggers adrenalin release. If this process is repeated enough, it is bad for mood, the heart, and other organ systems.[11]

Yet, stress is a natural part of life and cannot be avoided. One key to coping with stress is to recognize which specific situations act as stress triggers. If you can't steer clear of them altogether, you might need to do a lot of silent "self-talk" to get through them. According to psychologists and psychiatrists, it's always important to live one day at a time and to work one task at a time. Don't try to multitask, in itself a stressful activity.

Try not to be overly critical of yourself or others.

Try to be as flexible as possible when dealing with other people throughout the day. If plans change or someone suddenly has a conflict, and you're irritated, ask yourself how much it really matters to shift gears. Try not to be overly critical of yourself or others. Compassion, self-acceptance, and optimism can go a long way toward reducing the stress that one feels throughout the day.[12] For people recovering from any form of depression, controlling stress is the key to getting better. Stress leads to negative thinking and depression, all counter to a positive outlook. The following tips for coping with stress are from the nonprofit organization Mental Health America:

- Share your feelings with a friend if you feel stressed, anxious, or threatened.
- Visualize a very positive or peaceful scene while closing your eyes and breathing deeply. Really imagine every aspect of your surroundings from imagery to smells and sounds. Relax completely before opening your eyes again.
- If you are having a stressful day, take a break and find a quiet spot where you can meditate for a few minutes until you clear your mind.
- Remember that your doctor is a resource for you. If a stressful occurrence seems to be triggering an episode, contact him or her immediately and make an appointment.[13]

SAY
what

Mad Pride

A recent movement, fueled by the Internet, is the "coming out" of people with mood disorders, some of whom have documented their experiences on their own blogs. The movement, known as Mad Pride, has held marches and festivals in an attempt to ease the stigma of such conditions as bipolar disorder. "Until now, the acceptance of mental illness has pretty much stopped at depression," says Charles Barber, a lecturer in psychiatry at the Yale School of Medicine. "But a newer generation, fueled by the Internet . . . is saying, 'We deserve to be heard, too.'"[14]

One person with bipolar disorder who has spoken out honestly about her condition is Liz Spikol, a journalist in Philadelphia. Spikol is executive editor at *The Philadelphia Weekly*, where she chronicles her condition on a blog, which includes video clips called The Trouble with Spikol. Her blog comments on a wide array of topics, such as legislation related to mental health issues, the mood disorders of celebrities, and the pressures of "being a member of a minority group."

Other proponents of the Mad Pride movement are also speaking out in the hope that candor about their conditions will help their recoveries, provide a sense of community, and take some of the social condemnation away from their condition. "It used to be that you were labeled with your diagnosis and that was it; you were marginalized," says one woman who is an organizer for a mental health collective in Asheville, North Carolina. "If people found out, it was a death sentence, professionally and socially. We are hoping to change all that by talking."

THE CONTINUING DANGER OF SUICIDE

Surprisingly, the beginning of recovery from depression may be an increased time for risk of suicide. This seems contradictory. Why would alleviation of the worst symptoms of depression be a time for suicide? When depression lifts, people often experience a new surge of energy and sometimes use it to act out their suicidal thoughts and feelings. Anyone with a mood disorder is at a far greater lifetime risk for suicide, even if they have been treated for depression by a mental health professional and prescribed medication. In fact, 90 percent of people who commit suicide have a mental illness. Of that number, those who use alcohol or other drugs or exhibit disruptive or aggressive behavior are at the most risk.[15]

Suicide is a public health problem that claims 31,000 lives a year in the United States, with an additional 1.4 million people attempting suicide. This means that one person takes his or her own life every sixteen minutes. Suicide is not limited to adults. According to a 2004 study, an estimated 712,000 Americans between the ages of twelve and seventeen tried to kill themselves in that year. This number equals 2.9 percent of all Americans in that age range. Suicide rates have spiked in the last several decades. Between 1952 and 1996 the rate of suicide climbed by 14 percent for people in this same age group. Among African-American males aged fifteen to nineteen, the rate skyrocketed by 105 percent.[16]

An increase in suicide rates in the United States can be seen, too, in people in midlife. A 2008 analysis by the federal Centers for Disease Control and Prevention reported that the suicide rate among forty-five- to fifty-four-year-olds increased almost 20 percent from 1999 to 2004, the latest year studied. Although women have far lower suicide rates than men, their suicide rate increased dramatically—by 31 percent—according to the federal study. Experts seeking answers about the increase speculate that increased abuse of prescription drugs—and drug overdoses—is one possible explanation. Other possible causes include the growing pressures of life and the fraying of families and social networks.[17]

Causes of Suicide

Another reason that so many people with depression and bipolar disorder are at continual risk for suicide is medication "holidays," or lack of compliance with taking prescription medication. Some patients do not even fill their initial prescriptions, while others may not be able to afford the medications or might have trouble with side effects. The compliance rate—the amount that people stick with their medication regimen—is typically between 65 and 80 percent for patients who take antidepressant medication. It drops to 59 percent for lithium and 48 percent for valproic acid (Depakote).[18]

Working with a therapist is very helpful in encouraging people to stay on their medication. Also helpful are support groups or home visits (or followup phone calls) from mental health workers. Having an ongoing relationship with a mental health professional keeps awareness of mental illness and its hazards and complications "top of mind" with people. Equally important is teaching patients to recognize when their condition is worsening and what

Many people with depression and bipolar disorder are at continual risk for suicide because they do not take their prescription medication.

Complementary Medicine

Sometimes people with depression and bipolar disorder—as well as other illnesses—supplement the medicine prescribed by their physician with complementary medicine, which is nonconventional treatment, sometimes called alternative medicine. Popular types of complementary medicine include massage, acupuncture, aromatherapy, and *reiki*, a Japanese technique for stress reduction involving the redirection of energy flow of the body. Many types of complementary medicine, such as acupuncture and *reiki*, are Asian in origin.

Complementary medicine such as acupuncture is sometimes used to complement traditional treatments for depression and bipolar disorder.

Just a few decades ago, complementary medicine and traditional medicine occupied entirely different realms in the world of healing, but now nearly every major medical center across the United States encourages some form of complementary medicine to supplement traditional medical care. In 2000, Harvard Medical School launched a division to study complementary medicine and to conduct research about which types of complementary medicine

Continued on next page

Continued from previous page

were most effective. At the time Harvard's initiative began, approximately 42 percent of adults in the United States, about 82 million, routinely used complementary medicine therapies to treat their medical conditions, spending $27 billion on alternative medicines.[19] Unfortunately, some people try to replace modern medicine with complementary medicine altogether, which can hurt their health or aggravate a medical condition. Complementary medicine should never replace prescription medications and psychiatric treatment, but it can play a major role in reducing stress, which is paramount for anyone suffering from depression.

they can do to prevent a re-hospitalization or suicide attempt.[20] Again, this is why charting mood and promoting self-awareness of mood is so important.

Precautions Against Suicide

When someone seems to be in danger of committing suicide, all dangerous objects should be removed from their home, and their medications should be prescribed and dispensed to them in limited doses. Lithium, for example, can be fatal if taken in great quantities. Family and friends need to remember that the suicidal person's judgment is marred and they need others to act rationally and think for them during this difficult time. If someone has already had a suicide attempt or is given to suicidal depression, it's important to have an emergency plan in place detailing who will stay with the suicidal person, what hospital he or she will be taken to, which doctor will be contacted, who will care for any dependent children involved, and other details that would apply to a medical emergency.

Some warning signs for suicide are suicidal threats, withdrawing from others, moodiness, personality changes, uncharacteristically risky behavior, a personal crisis (such as a divorce, death, job loss, or other major setback), giving away possessions, and being at the beginning stage of recovery from a depressive episode.[21]

Family members and friends who believe that someone they know is in danger of committing suicide can implement the following precautions, recommended by The National Depressive and Manic-Depressive Association:

- Take talk of suicide seriously. Never say, "You'll feel better soon."
- Stay calm, but don't underreact.
- Involve other people. Don't handle the crisis on your own.
- Contact the person's psychiatrist or therapist and give concrete examples about why you feel your friend or family member is close to suicide.
- When talking to someone who is suicidal, engage them. Maintain eye contact and move close to them, even holding a hand if that is appropriate.
- Ask direct questions. Find out if your friend or family member has a specific plan for suicide.
- Acknowledge the person's feelings and never judge them.
- Reassure them they are not alone and tell them suicide is a permanent solution for a temporary problem.
- Don't promise confidentiality because you cannot provide that, and it would endanger the person's life.
- If possible, don't leave the person alone until he or she is in the hands of a professional(s).[22]

NEGATIVE THINKING AND ANGER

Suicidal depression is the most dramatic and dire outcome of continually negative thoughts and feelings. Self-loathing, worry, shame, and, especially, anger all contribute to negative thinking and depression. Not only can anger be psychologically destructive, it can wreak havoc on the body: The cardiovascular system, the endocrine system, and certainly human neurology all suffer when pent-up anger exists. Researchers have found that anger is concentrated in the region of the brain called the hypothalamus. But that insight doesn't really give someone either relief from anger or day-to-day guidance in how to handle it.[23]

One of the most important tools in coping with anger is learning how to make it less intense—quickly. First, identify what exactly is making you angry. Slow down and reflect. Having done this, allow a limited period of time, about two days, to feel upset and angry. Don't try to swallow the anger, which will only make it explode later on. During these two days, vent your anger to a sympathetic ear. After that, begin releasing the anger by writing in a journal, exercising, or doing some deep breathing.

Finally, and only after the anger is lessened, find a brief and non-abusive way to express your anger to the person who made you angry. "I" statements work well, such as "I felt angry when you said (or did) . . ." and then fill it in. If the person argues back, just say, "I guess we'll have to disagree about this" and walk away. Learning to release anger without being impulsive, destructive, or self-destructive is a priceless tool in balancing mood.[24]

BALANCING WORK, PLAY, AND REST

Feeling depressed can drain the joy from once pleasurable activities. The state of feeling that life lacks pleasure is called anhedonia. This is a feeling that leaves someone asking,

"Why bother to live?" Once a patient is stabilized on medication, it's important for him or her to create opportunities for pleasure. In fact, it's dire. Medication alone cannot balance the brain chemistry of depression and bipolar disorder. If someone who develops depression or bipolar disorder takes medication but lives in depressing circumstances or is isolated, she might relapse. Medication, sleep, food, and exercise must be supplemented with experiences that generate pleasure chemicals, such as serotonin, in the brain. These activities can be simple and free: a walk in the park, a book club, a community theater group, or a bike ride—all are critical in fighting depression.[25]

The state of feeling that life lacks pleasure is called anhedonia.

In times of stress or conflict, a wellness tool kit can come in handy. This is a simple box, a drawer, or a chest that contains items to help someone relax, reflect, and regain composure. A wellness tool kit might include an array of items for the body, mind, and spirit: an iPod with favorite music; a card from friends; pictures of best friends and family; a journal to reflect on the stresses of the day; a pair of sneakers for running or playing a sport; a DVD with a movie that makes you laugh; or a reminder of a special pet.[26]

If someone's days seem like an endless cycle of work, food, and sleep, then depression can loom large. The activities someone chooses should complement their new lifestyle and must exclude irregular hours, drinking alcohol, or illegal drug use. People should begin by scheduling pleasurable events once a week and then increasing the number to three or more if time permits.[27]

Of all the ways to spend free time, exercise ranks highest on the list. Researchers have proven that major depressive disorder improves with regular exercise and is helpful in the long-term management of the problem. Exercise improves self-perception, sleep, and physical discomforts, such as aches and pains. In one study, participants enrolled in an exercise program for two sixty-minute sessions a week that included a warm-up and a stretching, cool-down. There were twenty different types of exercise undertaken, for muscles throughout the body. Participants reported a more elevated mood, which researchers attributed to increased levels of the neurotransmitter serotonin.[28]

When Someone You Love Has Depression or Bipolar Disorder

Kay Redfield Jamison is the author of a textbook on bipolar disorder, a clinical psychologist and professor at a medical school—and someone who suffers from bipolar disorder. In her memoir, *An Unquiet Mind*, she recounts how her manic spending sprees became so uncontrollable that her brother had to intervene. Even he, with his PhD in economics from Harvard, found her piles of bills, bounced checks, letters from collection agencies, and late notices overwhelming. As Jamison recollects, it took her brother days to sort out the mess. After that, he took out a personal loan to pay Jamison's debt and relieve her of her financial troubles. Even after he flew home to Boston, across the country from Jamison's house in southern California, he called her continually to make sure she was okay, and frequently flew her to Boston to join him for weekends. An adult with a doctoral degree of her own, Jamison had become, in part, her brother's responsibility.[1]

The relationship between these two siblings illustrates one way that mental illness impacts a family: The needs of one person can spill over into other family members' lives. When mental illness affects one person in a family, no one stands untouched. Families divert resources such as time, physical energy, emotional

Depression and bipolar disorder can strain family relationships.

energy, and money into the task of caring for the sick family member. Often they repeat these efforts over the course of years, continually coping with emergencies, doctors, hospitalizations, and insurance companies. Family members, too, must survive the illness.

COPING WITH MOODS

Both depression and bipolar disorder pose challenges to relationships. It is painful and stressful to witness loved ones out of control or find them emotionally absent because of their illness. Seeing someone in a manic state is frightening because he or she can become abusive and even violent.

Both depression and bipolar disorder pose challenges to relationships.

Miranda,[2] a teenager, has a father with bipolar disorder. "I grew up with three fathers in the same person," she recalls. "The first was a very responsible and loving dad, really, a kind of perfect dad. He taught art at a local college and was very creative, so he would paint great murals on our bedroom walls or spend hours building a tree house that looked like a medieval castle in our back yard." She remembers her "second" dad as a scary person. "He was wound up and irritable," she says. "He stayed up all night and then when we were getting ready to go to school, he would go berserk if one of my brothers or I did the tiniest thing to annoy him. I remember he once screamed at my younger brother because he spilled a drop of orange juice on the counter when he was getting some breakfast. We had to be very careful around him, and we always felt afraid of him then." Miranda's "third" dad was her depressed dad. "He always managed to get himself to work, but as soon as he came home, he crawled into my parents' bedroom and didn't come out. Sometimes I wondered if he was still alive in there," she remembers. "My mother did her best to cope, but the behavior took a toll on all of us. Mom loved him and didn't want to leave him. Sometimes I'm glad and other times I wonder why she subjected me to that."

Miranda feels that one key to coping with her father's illness is realizing that he doesn't want to experience these changes in his mood. Being out of control and knowing that he is inflicting harm on his children is painful for him, too. Yet when he is experiencing mania, no amount of reasoning can bring him out of that state. This can be hard for the families of patients with bipolar disorder to accept.

People with mood disorders cannot pull themselves out of a given mental state any more easily than someone can overcome an epileptic seizure or a heart attack by will. Dismissing the feelings of someone with a mood disorder, telling them to "snap out of it" or to "pull yourself together" is futile and will only make matters worse. Family and friends of people with depression and bipolar disorder can only gain perspective on these diseases once they begin to understand and accept what their loved one is struggling with.

DENIAL

When mental illness first emerges, family members often want to blame the problems on individuals or external events: a bad breakup with a boyfriend or girlfriend, unfair teachers who are grading too harshly, police who too readily "bust a kid" for speeding or drug use. Some families know very little about mental illness,

It is critical that family members listen to each other's concerns.

Bipolar Disorder Affects Siblings, Too

Shawn[3], a young adult, recalls his experiences as the younger sibling of a bipolar brother. "My brother was in high school, and I was in elementary school. When he was sixteen and I was eleven, my life was turned upside down by him. All of a sudden, it was phone calls from the cops, asking my dad to pick him up: he was found with illegal drugs, he had crashed the car, and he had taken a swing at a teacher. My brother's illness was made worse because he was also a drug abuser. I think he frightened us all. He really made our lives hell for a few years. And during that time, I can't remember sitting down to dinner with my parents or feeling like part of a family. Holidays were the worst—almost like my brother had died, but was with us in the room. If it hadn't been for my best friend's family, I don't know what I would have done. They saw that I needed a safe haven and they kind of took me in for a while so my mom and dad could get through the next crisis."

Many teens with bipolar disorder have run-ins with law enforcement, especially during a manic phase.

With the help of therapy, Shawn finally admitted that he was bitter about the effect of his brother's illness on the family. "For a long time it made me angry, even though I know now that he couldn't help it. I felt that he exposed me to a lot of situations a little kid isn't ready for. I lost my big brother for a few years—and I also lost part of my childhood that I'll never get back."

while others know a lot in theory but have difficulty applying their knowledge to one of their own. Hillary[4] suffered from depression in high school and remembers well how her parents' denial almost cost her her life.

"I had been the classic good girl in high school," Hillary says. "I had straight A's, was the captain of the field hockey team, and in my parents' eyes I was heading for a top college," she recalls. "I have an older sister who was working two hours away in New York City, and I started calling her and telling her that I was crying all the time and felt so sad. I know she called my parents and tried to get me help, but my dad kept saying, 'It's just the pressure of junior year. She'll snap out of it.' It's like he thinks he would be a total failure if his kid went to see a psychiatrist. My sister came home for Thanksgiving and flipped out when she saw me," Hillary remembers. "I'd lost about fifteen or twenty pounds that fall because I just didn't feel like eating anything, and I was a stick. I remember her standing in the kitchen and really going at it with my dad and screaming at him for not getting me help. Then, she packed me into the car and drove me to the emergency room at the nearest medical center. My sister saved me."

Many families think that if stressors, like a demanding junior year of high school, can be removed, then the problem will always go away. Explanations like this serve two purposes: They direct the cause of the illness away from the family, and they make major depression seem temporary when, in fact, it is a genetic and lifelong health issue.[5]

STIGMA

One reason that families often deny the existence or severity of mental illness among them is stigma. People feel that if one family member is identified as having a mental disorder, the family is "marked" and its "shameful" secret will be revealed. The word "stigma" literally means to be branded. Unfortunately, many myths and misconceptions about mental illness persist. People who are depressed or have bipolar disorder may be seen as unreliable or somehow flawed

What Do You Say to Someone Who Is Depressed?

If someone you love has a mood disorder, avoid saying things that imply that he is at fault for his own condition. Words like "lazy" and "unmotivated" and "selfish" will only compound his problems with self-esteem. Instead, gently push him toward doing what is best, and offer your help along the way. Instead of saying, "All you do is lie around and eat junk food," offer to take a walk with him to get some sunshine and fresh air. Try to anticipate what events will arise and then choose some words and phrases in advance to help you through the situation:

- I know mornings are the hardest time of day for you. Let's go out for coffee and get a paper; we both need fresh air.
- You don't have to hide that you feel bad from me.
- Let's get some exercise together because I need it, too.[6]

by friends and neighbors who have little knowledge or sophistication about mental illness. Keeping the reality of the family a secret can result in isolation.

Miranda, whose father has bipolar disorder, remembers that as a child she didn't want to invite friends over in case her father spun out of control. She later learned that many of her school friend's parents had known about her father's condition and forbade their children from coming to her house. Miranda stopped receiving invitations to play with other kids because she was seen as somehow "tainted" by her father's illness—everyone kept their distance, isolating her and her siblings even more.

Isolation is ruinous to families with a mentally ill family member. These families need support, understanding, and extra help from friends, relatives, and neighbors—both emotional buttressing and aid with daily tasks such as shopping for food and cooking meals, keeping a household in order, and even filling out health insurance forms. A family's needs peak during times of crisis. If a parent is ill, who is going to take the kids to school and cook them dinner while the other parent copes? If a sibling is ill and needs the attention of both parents, who will comfort and care for the remaining children?

When someone they love is ill, families require extra support. Sadly, while communities often provide an outpouring of support for families coping with cancer or another chronic disease, they often back away from families impacted by mental illness because of the social stigma attached to emotional disorders.[7]

When someone they love is ill, families require extra support.

PROBLEMS WITHIN THE FAMILY

Living with someone who has depression or bipolar disorder creates serious challenges for all members of the family and can alter relationships between family members. The siblings of a teen with depression or bipolar disorder can suddenly find themselves sidelined as the parents turn all their attention to getting help for the ill child.[8] This can mean anything from spending nights with friends and neighbors to coping with the anger of feeling abandoned by parents. Other children in a family may feel jealous of the ill child because he or she is the "star" for the moment, receiving the bulk of the parents' attention.

The National Alliance on Mental Illness (NAMI) Family-to-Family Course

NAMI is the nation's largest advocacy group for people with mental illnesses with more than 1200 affiliates in the United States. The NAMI Family-to-Family course is a twelve-week educational program designed for a person whose family member has a mental illness.

Many people assume that they can get the best information about a loved one's mental illness from his or her physician. In fact, even the best doctors can never be absolutely certain that the medications they prescribe or the advice they dispense is the best for that patient. The family members are the ones who have the most extensive contact with him, so their understanding of the illness is critical. For these reasons, NAMI's Family-to-Family program has helped thousands of people augment knowledge that comes from a physician.

The program is run by people who have mentally ill loved ones. They go through a stringent training process and help families facing mental illness to cope and become more informed. People who go through the Family-to-Family program often report afterward that they feel more capable of taking care of their family members who were diagnosed with a mental illness. They do a better job communicating with physicians, school personnel, and the family member suffering from bipolar disorder. In addition, they can find coping skills to make their own lives more manageable in the face of chronic mental illness.[9]

A LIFE ON HOLD: CODEPENDENCY

Stolen years and a life on hold: These are frequently the price of living with a mentally ill person and coping with their ups and downs. Sometimes the burden can be too much to bear. Caregivers and family members may become angry, anxious, depressed, and exhausted. They can experience sleeplessness, irritability, lack of concentration, and even health problems as a result of the cumulative strain. The depression of one family member can be an engulfing force that is difficult to keep at bay.

Codependency is one of the most treacherous aspects of living with a mentally ill person, a drug addict, or an alcoholic (and these problems often coincide). People who are codependent have an overdeveloped and even inappropriate sense of responsibility for those around them. It's easier for them to become perpetual caretakers and to be concerned with others' feelings rather than their own. They aren't truly selfless, just numb to their own needs and automatically focused on those of others. Codependent people often confuse love with rescue or pity, which leads them down the road of ill-fated relationships.[10]

Codependency is one of the most treacherous aspects of living with a mentally ill person.

Casey grew up with a clinically depressed mother who "self-treated" her depression with alcohol. A current college student, she identifies herself as being a codependent person in her mother's recovery.

"No matter what I did growing up, my mom didn't get well, and I blamed myself on some level," Casey says. "I loved her and I hated her—and I always felt guilty about this. She was often drunk, and she was very dysfunctional. Thank God my father was a lawyer who earned a good living because he hired a great housekeeper who was there 24/7 to take care of me and my brother and make sure that Mom didn't burn down the house." Casey remembers being filled with so many confusing and powerful emotions that she was too

The depression of one family member can be difficult for everyone, especially codependent people.

young to handle and coping by feeling nothing. "I also latched onto every loser guy I could find trying to help him or make him happy. That's what I thought I deserved. I didn't even realize I was pretty. When I was voted 'Prettiest eyes' in high school, I almost fell over." Casey and her father both joined an Al-Anon group run by Alcoholics Anonymous. They found support and understanding there—and realized that depression, drug addiction, and alcoholism often co-exist as problems in families.[11]

Casey identifies herself as codependent but says that her father was not—and that saved her and her brother from even more emotional damage.

"After Mom began drinking heavily, Dad knew that if he stayed in the house, he'd be so worn out from dealing with her that he wouldn't have been able to take care of us," Casey remembers. "So he moved out and divorced her. He didn't want to drag my brother and me through a custody battle, so he bought a house down the block and set up another household there. We had his place, and Mom's place with her house-keeper/caretaker. If it weren't for my dad, my brother and I would have suffered much more."

SELF-CARE

Caregivers cannot fulfill their obligations to their families or to the mentally ill person unless they first take care of themselves. But how? In the middle of continual emotional, physical, and financial strain, it is still possible to maintain one's own physical and mental health with a concerted effort and creative trouble-shooting. Positive steps toward self-care include:

- Enlisting help. Caregivers should learn to rely on others. Get people to share in the responsibilities. By hiring a housekeeper, Casey's father brought in another adult to help care for his ex-wife and raise his children.
- Accept your feelings. Mental illness is stressful and unpleasant. It produces feelings of anger and frustration in loved ones and can create rifts in families and even within a single person. Half of that person may want to flee while the other half wants to stay and help. Sitting on feelings only makes them explode. Casey's father accepted the fact that he could no longer live with her mother and survive, so he crafted an imaginative solution by moving just down the block. If he had forced himself to remain in the house, his anger and frustration might have made the home environment even more toxic.
- Seek advice and support. Support groups and well-qualified therapists abound. A good place to start is with a well-known national or local support group with a good reputation. Medical centers often provide support groups for families of behavioral health patients. They also provide referrals to psychiatrists, psychologists, and mental health workers.
- Take time for yourself. When a family is coping with a mentally ill person, they can set aside basic needs such as healthy eating, sleep, exercise, and positive socializing. In fact, self-care is most important during times of intense stress. Even a half-hour walk a day, a fruit or vegetable with every meal, and lots of water can do wonders for increasing stamina and improving mood.[12]

College Counseling Helps

Because bipolar disorder frequently emerges in the late teens and early twenties, it often coincides with the time when most people have recently graduated from high school and are beginning college or a full-time job. This time of life is a huge adjustment for adolescents. They are on their own for the first time, with less supervision and support from their parents. For someone who has bipolar disorder, the lifestyle of a young adult can be a significant challenge—and is the opposite of what they need to be healthy. Late hours and easy access to illegal drugs and alcohol are dangerous for a person with bipolar disorder. Irregular hours alone can trigger an incident.

A student who begins to feel depressed or manic can turn to the counseling center at the college or university for help. Counseling centers are staffed by trained professionals with experience working with young adults who face mental health issues. This is a good place for a college

The onset of bipolar disorder frequently coincides with the time when most people have recently graduated high school and are beginning college or a full-time job.

student in crisis to turn as a first step. It can be confusing for family members to try to sort out what is happening with a college student with bipolar disorder, especially if they are communicating over the phone. If parents can convince a student to come home so the family can assess the situation in conjunction with a mental health professional, the face-to-face contact often eases the family's worries.

READINESS

Once a family has taken initiative to cope with depression or bipolar disorder (or other mental illness), there are some concrete steps that will enable everyone involved to feel more prepared to handle the ongoing situation, which may include moments of crisis. Neatly write or type key contact numbers and post them on the refrigerator or bulletin board. These numbers should

Neatly writing or typing a list of key contact numbers and posting them on the refrigerator will help if a crisis arises.

include a physician, a local hospital, trusted neighbors, friends and family, and a pharmacy. Locating a twenty-four-hour pharmacy is always helpful in case a psychiatrist needs to phone in a prescription.

Keep a written record of all the medications and dosages your loved one is receiving. On the same sheet, note any special dietary instructions. For example, lithium should be taken with food or it will produce nausea.

Keep a written record of all the medications and dosages your loved one is receiving.

The ability to identify your loved one's moods before they peak is very helpful. On a small notepad, write down the warning signs of depression or mania, including any special words or behaviors. The onset of mania can be signaled by irritability, rapid speech, new projects, late hours, and grand dreams and schemes.[13]

People heading into mania often use more profanity or sexually explicit language while those nose-diving into depression might experience a bout of hypersomnia, sleeping unusually long hours. Writing down your loved one's behaviors will help you recognize these signs and symptoms more easily when they reappear.

You should also keep a list of day-to-day chores that you can pass off to a willing volunteer. If someone says, "What can I do to help?" just read from your list and let him or her choose a task like making a dinner, walking the dog, babysitting a child, or mowing a lawn.[14]

YOUNG ADULTS WITH BIPOLAR DISORDER

Because the onset of bipolar disorder is frequently during late adolescence or early twenties, special issues arise. This is normally a time of increased independence. Most people of this age are moving away from home and attending college, working, sharing an apartment, working their way through school, or making other strides toward independence. Bipolar disorder disrupts these steps toward autonomy because parents are suddenly thrown into the role of caretaker once more. The new twist on the relationship raises many questions. Should young adults with bipolar disorders be supported financially by their parents? Should they live with them or is it better if a parent helps fund an apartment for the child? Should a parent be the one to remind a young adult who has bipolar disorder to take medication?

There is no single answer to these questions because family finances, the severity of the child's illness, and the parents' emotional resources all help determine what arrangement works best for each family. Remembering that a young adult with bipolar disorder must be treated as a young adult and not as a child is important. So, too, is preserving the home as a haven. If the young adult with bipolar disorder is abusing drugs, behaving erratically, or refusing to take medication, it might be better for him or her to be in a more professionally therapeutic setting, such as a psychiatric hospital or a day program.[15]

Outlook for the Future

Today, psychiatrists continue to explore the human mind. Research into depression, bipolar disorder, and other mental illnesses is one of the most dynamic fields of medicine. In laboratories across the world, scientists delve into the structure of the brain, the specific genes that carry markers for mental illness, and the relationship between addiction and mental illness.

However, intellectual discovery inside a research facility or university-sponsored clinic is only the beginning of developing the treatment a patient typically receives in a doctor's office. At research centers, experiments and long-term studies abound. Not all the discoveries issuing from them are adopted by physicians as part of a standard of care, but new hope for better lives begins in research facilities at major universities across the globe. Eventually, some of these advances are incorporated into standard psychiatric practice. Then, individuals suffering from various types of depression benefit from the research and find relief.

RESEARCH ABOUT DEPRESSION AND BIPOLAR DISORDER

World-renowned McLean Hospital is a Harvard-affiliated institution that has earned a global reputation for research into and treatment of mental illness. Its purpose and activities have changed dramatically since its founding as the McLean Insane Asylum in the nineteenth century, mirroring the revolution in treatment of mental and mood disorders. The wide variety of studies undertaken there today is among the most impressive in the world. The projects at McLean give a glimpse into cutting-edge research by the top physicians and scientists in the field of psychiatric disorders.[1]

One team of researchers at McLean Hospital is working to pinpoint the specific genes that are expressed as bipolar disorder in genetically suspectible individuals. The goal of the research is to find drug treatments that are more effective than current drugs. To accomplish this, bipolar disorder and schizophrenia must be better understood on the level of genes, cells, and molecules.

One research team explored an area of the brain called the hippocampus, which is responsible for learning and memory. They found that people with bipolar disorder have defects in the functioning of certain cells within the hippocampus that release an amino acid known as aminobutyric acid or GABA. This amino acid (a protein) helps control the flow of information in the brain and it plays an important role in regulating "excitability" throughout the cells in the nervous system. This type of research sheds light on why a brain with bipolar disorder produces different behavior than that of a normal brain.[2]

Another Harvard-sponsored project researches new treatments for patients who suffer from both bipolar disorder and alcohol dependence or substance abuse. The study specifically focuses on women in order to determine whether or not there are gender differences that are significant in the recovery from both conditions. Researchers for this project are especially interested in which combinations of medication and psychotherapy work best for women grappling with both mental illness and drug addiction. Research is still ongoing.[3]

The start of the twenty-first century began a new era in child psychiatry. Before that, most physicians thought that mental illness never emerged before adolescence and young adulthood. Later, the idea of childhood mental illness was reevaluated. It's now understood that children as young as four years old can display the symptoms of bipolar disorder. In fact, studies to explore mental illness have been known to include patients in preschool through those in college.

One such study that began in 2004 looked at the overlap between ADHD and bipolar disorder in children and young adults. The study looked at why these conditions often occur in the same child. Researchers wondered if there was an underlying problem with the structure of the brain that in some way contributed to these co-existing problems. Using magnetic resonance imaging (MRI), the researchers were able to see inside the brain's structures and discovered that the brains of children with ADHD and bipolar disorder actually appear to be different from the brains of children without these symptoms or any family history of these illnesses.[4]

Old age was the focus of a 2006 study conducted at Mount Sinai School of Medicine in New York. There, researchers found that a history of depression was associated with an

A patient prepares to undergo an MRI. Researchers are using magnetic resonance imaging (MRI) to study the brain structures of mentally ill patients.

increase in Alzheimer's disease and rapid decline in the ability to think and reason in old age. Researchers looked carefully at pathways in the neurons and concluded that both major depressive disorder and Alzheimer's disease were likely to affect the brain's memory-related temporal lobes.[5]

To advance the field of psychiatry, researchers have studied many categories of people affected by mental illness: the very young, the very old, women, men, drug addicts, those with family histories of bipolar disorder/depression, and those without. Scientists have explored the biological triggers that "turn on" a depressive state. They have looked at biological markers on individual genes. They've also tried to assess the genetic transmission of risk factors and peered into the brain to identify how depression changes the appearance of the brain through neuroimaging. Scientists have studied animal models and they have tried to narrow down the reasons why the depressed brain responds better to some drugs than to others. This exhaustive exploration of mood and the brain is one of the most exciting and hopeful avenues in science today. Research into depression and bipolar disorder is critical for the continued well-being of our society because mental illness is so widespread.

DEPRESSION AND SOCIETY

Without mental health, there can be no society. Families, communities, schools, hospitals, and workplaces all rely on people who are clear-thinking, energetic, productive, and responsible. Without medication to combat symptoms, both depression and bipolar disorder impair consistent functioning. These conditions can make a daily routine and the realization of goals nearly impossible to achieve. Untreated, they constitute a threat to our well-being as a community, as well as individually.

Unfortunately, mental illness is common both in the United States and around the world. Each year, physicians diagnose one in four Americans with a recognized mental illness, or about 57.7 million people, according to the 2004 U.S. census. Nearly half of that number suffers from more than one mental illness at a time. According to major international healthcare groups, including the World Health Organization, the economic impact of mental illness across the globe is greater than that of cancer.[6]

WHO IS MOST VULNERABLE?

People living amid racism, discrimination, violence, and poverty have the highest rates of mental illness, according to a report issued by the surgeon general of the United States in 2000. In fact, those living with the lowest amount of income and education are two to three times more likely to suffer from mental illness than those at the top of the society.[7] Why? Living in poverty produces stress and repeated stress can worsen or even cause mental illness. At the same time, people in poorer neighborhoods often lack access to high-quality health care of any type, including mental health care.

People living amid racism, discrimination, violence, and poverty have the highest rates of mental illness, according to a report issued by the surgeon general of the United States in 2000.

Several groups suffer most from the lack of adequate health care. Mental health services are not always available in their community. In some cases, language barriers make communication with professionals too difficult. For many groups, mental illness is still a shameful occurrence. Individuals feel embarrassed to address the problems they're having. The people most lacking critical mental health services include: African Americans, American Indians and Alaska Natives, Asian Americans and Pacific Islanders, and Hispanic Americans.[8]

A BRIGHTER FUTURE

Currently, there are large and unfair differences between the mental health services available to the underprivileged and those available to Americans with more resources. Yet, change and improvement are possible with adequate government support. To dramatically reduce depression in the U.S., researchers have to conduct large-scale investigations into the needs of various communities. Treatments and services that would be most effective for Asians, for example, might not work as well with Latinos because culture shapes each group's response to mental illness. Research studies need to determine the best way for mental health professionals from outside a group to work with an ethnic community and have a positive result for their efforts rather than being viewed as outsiders.[9]

In addition to determining needs, mental health professionals can improve access to treatment and delivery of services. One way of doing this is to make mental health care an overall part of health and not segregate it into a separate category. For example, when a mother takes an infant to a clinic for a checkup or shots, she can also be evaluated for postpartum depression continually. Another important step might

Depression and Professional Football

Who suffers from depression? The question brings to mind a wide array of people: teenagers, mothers of newborns, and even glamorous celebrities such as rock stars and actors. Athletes don't usually number among this group in the popular imagination because they're seen as vigorous and powerful, especially professional athletes who earn salaries that most people could only dream about. A recent study has debunked the myth that one group of star athletes live depression-free: football players.

Why would football players, especially those who have retired, be prone to depression? The answer is both obvious and startling. Pro football players suffer more concussions than other athletes, in general. In fact, three or more severe concussions aren't unusual during the course of a career in the National Football League.

In 2007, a study appearing in a journal of the American College of Sports Medicine linked concussion to both depression and the early onset of Alzheimer's disease. A poll of more than 2,500 football players revealed that of the 595 who had sustained three or more concussions during play, 20 percent had problems with depression. This is a significant percentage. The poll provoked an uproar in the world of professional football—and it also has significance for society. Americans are sports enthusiasts and nearly every school district or town recreational program in the United States offers football to children as young as eight. The knowledge that head injuries can lead to depression may have widespread consequences in secondary school and college athletic programs in the future.[10]

Recent studies show that football players who suffered from three or more concussions were more likely to suffer from depression.

be to identify which patients are most vulnerable to mental illness and begin delivery of care before a problem develops. This could involve identifying children in foster care or those whose parents are in drug treatment programs, and then supporting them with individual or group therapy as a preventative measure.

Two other important steps to significantly reduce mental illness in the U.S. include reducing the cost of care and the stigma attached to mental illness. Uninsured Americans have virtually no way of receiving quality health care of any sort, especially mental health care, unless they enter a hospital through the emergency room. This is an expensive and wasteful route to mental health care. Satellite mental health programs, established by major medical centers and community hospitals in surrounding neighborhoods, could provide higher-quality care and also raise the profile of mental health. In addition, satellite programs could offer educational programs to schools, religious groups, and families.[11]

VETERANS AND MENTAL HEALTH

Veterans returning from combat face some of the toughest mental health problems. Fighting in hostile terrain for months—and even years—at a time can make even the most mentally stable person stressed and depressed. Major depression, anxiety, and post-traumatic stress disorder (PTSD) are among the most common mental health problems suffered by U.S. soldiers. A 2008 article in *Time* magazine reported on the new use of Prozac and other antidepressants by American soldiers during combat. The medication was prescribed by military physicians to help soldiers cope with the stress of battle. The article concluded that because tours of duty are often extended, soldiers serving in Iraq and Afghanistan have had insufficient time to recover from their experiences in war before returning home. The leaves of soldiers are too brief for them to be able to "bounce back" from the stress of wartime and there is a "significant risk of mental health problems" in these soldiers and that risk was caused by both poor access to medical care and by the reluctance of soldiers to seek it because of the stigma involved.[12]

Fighting in hostile terrain for months—and even years—at a time can make even the most mentally stable person stressed and depressed.

The article noted that untreated PTSD in returning solders has "immediate implications" for the society, meaning that as solders return home their state of mental health will impact U.S. society at once.[13]

WHAT THE FUTURE HOLDS

Each day, researchers around the country make new discoveries about the causes, diagnosis, and treatment of depression and bipolar disorder. These findings are released to the nation's approximately 38,000 psychiatrists through articles in professional journals, lectures, and at the annual meeting of the American Psychiatric Association. Often the road from lab to patient is a long one, because new ideas need to be refined over time. Since the 1970s, there has been huge growth in the number of research labs in the United States studying mental illness. During the same period, society has become more accepting of depression and bipolar disorder as physically based diseases. Recently, the government has mandated that

People with depression and bipolar disorder can still lead fulfilling lives as long as they do their best to stay positive and not let their symptoms overwhelm their daily lives and activities.

insurance companies, too, treat these problems as medical conditions and not place them in a separate category. Yet, despite significant advances in the field of psychiatry, people with depression and bipolar disorder have *treatable*, but not *curable* conditions. The medications they take alleviate their symptoms, but do not change the root cause. Like those living with diabetes, epilepsy, or many other illnesses, people who have depression and bipolar disorder must work on living a life that attends to their body, mind, and spirit in order to achieve balance and stability.

Depression and Bipolar Disorder Timeline

460–379 B.C.: The Greek physician Hippocrates, widely regarded as the father of medicine, disputes the view that emotional disorders are the result of the gods' displeasure or of possession by demons. He claims that emotional disorders have physical causes, just like other diseases.

280 B.C.: The philosopher Theophrastus writes *The Characters*, in which he puts to use his observations of people to create a detailed list of "natures bad," and describes twenty-eight disorders of the personality.

23–79 A.D.: Pliny the Elder, a Roman who studied nature, writes several volumes about the healing powers of plants and herbs, including those that can treat mental illness.

1000: Soranus of Ephesus, a Roman physician working in Alexandria, Egypt, primarily as a gynecologist and obstetrician, prescribes mineral water therapy for mania; the nearby springs turn out to be rich in the salt lithium. Avicenna, an Arabian philosopher known as a writer on medicine and other sciences, writes a long paper exploring the relationship between the body and the soul and the causes of melancholy (depression). He advocates for humane treatment of the insane.

1100: At Metz in France, the first recorded institution for the mentally ill is founded.

1300: During the Black Death, one-third of the world's population from India to Iceland is wiped out. In the face of this calamity, superstition once again supersedes science. The mentally ill are treated by "casting out the devils" within them, sometimes with torture or burning at the stake.

1403: Outside London, England, the institution named St. Mary of Bethlehem or "Bedlam," as it was called, is founded and treats psychiatric patients.

1500s: Intolerance of the mentally ill intensifies. They are seen as a danger to the public because they "carry the devil" inside them. Public burnings claim the lives of hundreds across Europe and thousands more die by other methods at the hands of mobs, executioners, or torturers.

1547: St. Mary of Bethlehem (Bedlam) moves to London and focuses solely on the treatment of psychiatric patients.

1758: In Britain, William Battie, an English physician, publishes the first book on the care of the mentally ill, in which he advocates a therapeutic approach. His work *Treatment on Madness* brought the slang word for madness, "batty," into use.

1812: In the United States, Benjamin Rush, a doctor in Philadelphia, compiles his observations of mental illness and publishes *Medical Inquiries and Observations upon the Disease of the Mind*—the only and thereby the definitive text on psychiatric care for the next seventy years.

1880: Data from the U.S. census is used to define categories of mental illness among Americans. Seven categories are created: mania, melancholia, monomania, paresis, dementia, dipsomania, and epilepsy.

1890: Harvard professor William James publishes an exploration of the functions of the human brain *Principles of Psychology*, a landmark study. James was a pioneer in psychology and helped found it as a legitimate science.

1895–1900: In Vienna, Freud writes and publishes two important works that help launch the psychoanalytic movement: *Studies on Hysteria* (1900) and *The Interpretation of Dreams* (1895). Psychoanalysis emphasized the importance of sexual development in people's psychological lives. Freud had theories about depression, all of which were psychologically rather than physically based.

1917: As the United States enters World War I, the military for the first time has an awareness of the new science of psychology and the tools to screen recruits for psychological problems with a series of tests to detect "abnormal" behavior.

1921: The American Psychiatric Association is formed.

1933: Manfred J. Sakel introduces coma therapy as a treatment for schizophrenia.

1934: Electroconvulsive therapy (ECT) is first introduced in Hungary by von Meduna, but does not produce reliable results.

1935: Yale University professor John Fulton demonstrates before colleagues the changed and calm behavior of two chimpanzees that had undergone frontal lobe removal. Antonio Moniz performs the first leucotomy on a female patient, destroying the fibers connecting her frontal lobes to the rest of her brain.

1938: Electroconvulsive therapy (ECT) refined in Italy by Ugo Cerletti and Lucio Bini and used more widely in Europe and the United States.

1948: First "ice-pick" lobotomy performed by Walter Freeman.

1949: Australian psychiatrist J.F.J. Cade uses lithium to stabilize mood and quiet the symptoms of psychosis.

1952: Publication of the first edition of the bible of psychiatry, the DSM-1—the *Diagnostic and Statistical Manual of Mental Disorders.* French researchers discover the drug chlorpromazine can be used to prevent psychosis, and the field of psychopharmacology is born.

1960s: Tricyclic antidepressants and monoamine oxidase inhibitors (MAOIs) first come into use.

1970: The Food and Drug Administration approves lithium for use in the United States.

1970s–90s: Researchers and doctors engage in the development and clinical use of selective serotonin reuptake inhibitors (SSRIs).

2000s: MRIs and PET scans are used to look inside the brain and see structural differences in bipolar brains.

2008: Congress passes "parity" law mandating that insurance companies treat mental illness and physical illness by the same standard.

Chapter Notes

What Are Depression and Bipolar Disorder?

1. National Institute of Mental Health, "The Numbers Count: Mental Disorders in America," August 10, 2009, <http://www.nimh.nih.gov/health/publications/the-numbers-count-mental-disorders-in-america/index.shtml> (September 30, 2009).

2. Ibid.

3. Ibid.

4. Mayo Foundation for Medical Education and Research, *Mayo Clinic on Depression: Answers to Help You Understand, Recognize and Manage Depression*, 1st ed., ed. Keith Kramlinger, MD (Rochester, Minn.: Mayo Clinic Health Information, 2001), Vol. 1, p. 18.

Introduction

1. Sara Kershaw, "The Murky Politics of Mind-Body," *The New York Times*, March 30, 2008, <http://www.nytimes.com/2008/03/30/weekinreview/30kers.html> (September 30, 2009).

2. National Institute of Mental Health, "The Numbers Count: Mental Disorders in America," August 10, 2009, <http://www.nimh.nih.gov/health/publications/the-numbers-count-mental-disorders-in-america/index.shtml> (September 30, 2009).

3. Ibid.

Chapter 1: Straight Talk About Depression and Bipolar Disorder

1. Patient composite is drawn from interviews with psychiatrists who are attending physicians at medical centers in New Jersey and New York (March—July 2008).

2. Kay Redfield Jamison, *An Unquiet Mind* (New York: Vintage Books, 1995), p. 150.

3. Rand Corporation, "One in Five Iraq and Afghanistan Veterans Suffer From PTSD or Major Depression," April 17, 2008, <http://www.rand.org/news/press/2008/04/17/> (September 30, 2009).

4. Depression and Bipolar Support Alliance, "Rising Toll of Depression Measured in Disability, Death and Dollars, Landmark Mental Health Report Finds," April 17, 2008, <http://www.dbsalliance.org/pdfs/wppressrelease.pdf> (September 30, 2009).

5. Mayo Foundation for Medical Research and Education, *Mayo Clinic on Depression: Answers to Help You Understand, Recognize and Manage Depression*, 1st ed., ed. Keith Kramlinger, MD (Rochester, Minn.: Mayo Clinic Health Information, 2001), Vol. 1, p. 18.

6. The Office of Applied Studies, Substance Abuse and Mental Health Services Administration, National Survey on Drug Use and Health (NSDUH) Report, "Suicidal Thoughts among Youths Aged 12 to 17 with Major Depressive Episodes," September 9, 2005, <http://www.oas.samhsa.gov/2k5/suicide> (September 30, 2009).

7. Ibid.

8. National Institute of Mental Health, "Rates of Bipolar Diagnosis in Youth Rapidly Climbing, Treatment Patterns Similar to Adults," 2007, <http://www.nimh.nih.gov/science-news/2007/rates-of-bipolar-diagnosis-in-youth-rapidly-climbing-treatment-patterns-similar-to-adults.shtml> (September 30, 2009).

9. National Institute of Mental Health, "Bipolar Spectrum Disorder May be Under-recognized and Improperly Treated," 2007, <http://www.nimh.nih.gov/science-news/2007> (September 30, 2009).

10. Jerrold F. Rosenbaum, MD, "New Clinical Advances in Depression," May 15, 2001, <http://www.medscape.com/viewarticle/420245> (September 30, 2009).

11. Depression and Bipolar Support Alliance, "The State of Depression in America," April 17, 2008, <http://www.dbsalliance.org/pdfs/wplowres.pdf> (September 30, 2009).

12. Ronald R. Fieve, MD, *Moodswing*, 2nd ed., rev. (New York: Bantam Books, 1997), pp. 283–287.

13. Jen C. Wang, et al., "Evidence of common and specific genetic effects: association of the muscarinic acetylcholine receptor M2 (CHRM2) gene with alcohol dependence and major depressive syndrome," *Human Molecular Genetics*, September 1, 2004, pp. 1903–1911.

14. Real Mental Health, "Celebrities with Depression," October 2008, <http://www.realmentalhealth.com/depression/depression_celebs.asp> (September 30, 2009).

Chapter 2: History of Depressive Disorders

1. U.S. Census Bureau, "Census of Population and Housing: 1840 Census," n.d., <http://www.census.gov/prod/www/abs/decennial/1840.htm> (September 30, 2009).

2. Ann Palmer, "20th Century History of the Treatment of Mental Illness: A Review," December 14, 2008 <http://www.mnpsychsoc.org/history%20appendix.pdf> (September 30, 2009).

3. Ibid.

4. Ibid.

5. Ibid.

6. Ibid.

7. Renato M.E. Sabbatini, PhD, "The History of Shock Therapy in Psychiatry," n.d., <http://www.cerebromente.org.br/n04/historia/shock_i.htm> (September 30, 2009).

8. Palmer.

9. R. L. Spitzer, "The diagnostic status of homosexuality in DSM-III: a reformulation of the issues," *The American Journal of Psychiatry*, April 23, 1981, <http://ajp.psychiatryonline.org/cgi/content/abstract/138/2/210> (September 30, 2009).

10. American Psychiatric Association, *DSM-IV* (Arlington, Va.: American Psychiatric Publishing, Inc., 2000), pp. 124–138.

11. Sabbatini.

12. Ibid.

13. Joel Braslow, *Psychiatric Treatment in the first Half of the 21st Century: Mental Ills and Bodily Cures* (Berkeley and Los Angeles: University of California Press, 1995), p. 94.

14. Bengt Jansson, "Controversial Psychosurgery Resulted in a Nobel Prize," October 29, 1998, <http://nobelprize.org/nobel_prizes/medicine/articles/moniz/index.html> (September 30, 2009).

15. Ibid.

16. Ibid.

17. Ibid.

18. Pete Earley, "Living with Mental Illness," *USA Today*, May 1, 2006, <http://www.usatoday.com/news/opinion/editorials/2006-05-01-mental-illness_x.htm> (September 30, 2009).

19. Jansson.

20. John Crilly, MD, "The history of clozapine and its emergence in the U.S. market," *History of Psychiatry*, Vol. 18, no. 1, (2007), pp. 39–60.

21. Ibid.

22. The Treatment Advocacy Center, "Resources: Quick Facts," 2009, <http://www.treatmentadvocacycenter.org/GeneralResources/index.php?option=com_content&task=view&id=100&Itemid=123> (September 30, 2009).

23. Ronald R. Fieve, MD, *Moodswing*, 2nd ed., rev. (New York: Bantam Books 1997), pp. 60–62.

24. Ibid.

25. Kay Redfield Jamison, *An Unquiet Mind* (New York: Vintage Books, 1995), p. 80.

26. Ibid.

27. The Mayo Clinic: "Depression: Selective Serotonin Reuptake Inhibitors (SSRIs)," December 10, 2008 <http://www.mayoclinic.com/health/ssris/MH00066> (September 30, 2009).

28. Fieve, p. 65.

Chapter 3: The Science of Depression and Bipolar Disorder

1. Tara W. Strine, et al., "Depression and anxiety in the United States: Findings from the 2006 Behavioral Risk Factor Surveillance System," *Psychiatric Services*, December 2008, Vol. 59, pp. 1383–1390.

2. Ibid.

3. Robert Ornstein and Richard F. Thompson, *The Amazing Brain* (Boston: Houghton Mifflin Company, 1976), pp. 21–41.

4. Ibid.

5. Ibid.

6. Ibid.

7. Ibid.

8. Frank I. Tarazi and John A. Schetz, "Neurological and Psychiatric Disorders From Bench to Bedside," *Current Clinical Neurology*, November 17, 2007, <http://springerlink.com/content/m6n245115mmg1653/?p=ac2dae197120450 abbd955d77f07133d&pi=9> (September 30, 2009).

9. Mayo Foundation for Medical Research and Education, *Mayo Clinic on Depression: Answers to Help You Understand, Recognize and Manage Depression*, 1st ed., ed. Keith Kramlinger, MD (Rochester, Minn.: Mayo Clinic Health Information, 2001), Vol. 1, p. 31.

10. Ibid.

11. Ibid.

12. Endocrineweb.com, "How your Thyroid Works," May 21, 2009, <http://www.endocrineweb.com/thyfunction.html> (September 30, 2009).

13. Ibid.

14. The National Women's Health Information Center, "Depression During and After Pregnancy," March 6, 2009, <http://www.womenshealth.gov/faq/postpartum.htm#2> (September 30, 2009).

15. Mayo Foundation for Medical Education and Research, pp. 129–131.

16. Brooke Shields, "War of Words," *The New York Times*, July 1, 2005, <http://www.nytimes.com/2005/07/01/opinion/01shields.html> (September 30, 2009).

17. Ibid.

18. Michael H. Elbert, Peter T. Loosen, and Barry Nurcomb, *Current Diagnosis and Treatment in Psychiatry* (New York: Lange Medical Books/McGraw-Hill, 2000), p. 291.

19. Sara Kershaw, "The Murky Politics of Mind-Body," *The New York Times*, March 8, 2006, <http://www.nytimes.com/2008/03/30/weekinreview/30kers.html> (September 30, 2009).

20. Jen C. Wang, et al., *Human Molecular Genetics*, September 1, 2004, Vol. 13, pp. 1903–1911.

21. Mayo Foundation for Medical Education and Research, pp. 129–131.

22. National Institute of Mental Health, "The Numbers Count: Mental Disorders in America," August 10, 2009, <http://www.nimh.nih.gov/health/publications/the-numbers-count-mental-disorders-in-america/index.shtml#Mood> (September 30, 2009).

23. Jennifer Egan, "The Bipolar Puzzle," *The New York Times*, September 12, 2008, <http://www.nytimes.com/2008/09/14/magazine/14bipolar-t.html?_r=1&scp=1&sq=Kiki+Chang&st=nyt> (September 14, 2008).

24. Patient composite is drawn from interviews with psychiatrists who are attending physicians at medical centers in New Jersey and New York (March—July 2008).

Chapter 4: Identifying Depression and Bipolar Disorder

1. National Institute of Mental Health, "The Numbers Count: Mental Disorders in America," August 10, 2009, <http://www.nimh.nih.gov/health/publications/the-numbers-count-mental-disorders-in-america/index.shtml#Mood> (September 30, 2009).

2. Ibid.

3. Ibid.

4. Ibid.

5. Ibid.

6. Alan Langlieb, MD, "Mental Illness Exacts 'Enormous Toll' on U.S. Businesses and Institutions, Hopkins Psychiatrist Finds," November 10, 2000, <http://www.hopkinsmedicine.org/Press_releases/2005/11_10_05.html> (September 30, 2009).

7. Mayo Foundation for Medical Education and Research, *Mayo Clinic On Depression: Answers to Help You Understand, Recognize, and Manage Depression*, 1st ed., ed. Keith Kramlinger, MD (Rochester, Minn.: Mayo Clinic Health Information, 2001), p. 18.

8. Harvard Health Publications, "Depression in Children and Teenagers," May 3, 2008, <http://www.health.harvard.edu/newsweek/Depression_in_Children_and_Teenagers.htm> (September 30, 2009).

9. National Institute of Mental Health, "Suicide In the U.S.: Statistics and Prevention," July 27, 2009, <http://www.nimh.nih.gov/health/publications/suicide-in-the-us-statistics-and-prevention/index.shtml> (September 30, 2009).

10. National Institute of Mental Health, "Rates of Bipolar Diagnosis in Youth Rapidly Climbing, Treatment Patterns Similar to Adults," September 3, 2007, <http://www.nimh.nih.gov/science-news/2007/rates-of-bipolar-diagnosis-in-youth-rapidly-climbing-treatment-patterns-similar-to-adults.shtml> (September 30, 2009).

11. Demitri Papolos, MD and Janice Papolos, *The Bipolar Child: The Definitive and Reassuring Guide to Childhood's Most Misunderstood Disease* (New York: Random House, 1999), p. 128.

12. David J. Milkowitz, *The Bipolar Disorder Survival Guide* (New York: The Guilford Press, 2002), p. 47.

13. Kay Redfield Jamison, *An Unquiet Mind* (New York: Vintage Books, 1995), p. 80.

14. Milkowitz, p. 47.

15. National Alliance on Mental Illness, "Mental Illnesses: Bipolar Disorder," October 2006, <http://www.nami.org/Template.cfm?Section=By_Illness& Template=/TaggedPage/TaggedPageDisplay.cfm&TPLID=54&ContentID= 23037> (September 30, 2009).

16. Joseph A. Lehrer, et al., "Depressive Symptoms as a Longitudinal Predictor of Sexual Risk Behaviors Among U.S. Middle and High School Students," *Pediatrics*, July 2006, Vol. 118, pp. 189–200.

17. Ibid.

18. Ibid.

19. Hillary Smith, "Bipolar Disorder Risk Factors for Suicide: Which Factors Increase A Bipolar Patient's Risk of Suicide," June 17, 2009, <http://suicide.suite101.com/article.cfm/bipolar_disorder_risk_factors_for_ suicide#ixzz0QwUJZLOF> (September 30, 2009).

20. Jamison, p. 80.

21. Patient composite is drawn from interviews with psychiatrists who are attending physicians at medical centers in New Jersey and New York (March—July 2008).

22. Mental Health America, "Factsheet: Depression and Teens," n.d., <http://www.mentalhealthamerica.net/go/information/get-info/depression/ depression-in-teens> (September 30, 2009).

23. Mayo Foundation for Medical Education and Research, pp. 129–131.

24. Ibid.

25. Ibid.

26. Joey Bartolomeo, "Living with Mental Illness," *U.S. Weekly*, April 14, 2008, p. 60.

Chapter 5: Treatment of Depression and Bipolar Disorder

1. Depression and Bipolar Support Alliance, "You've Just Been Diagnosed…" November 26, 2007, <http://www.dbsalliance.org/site/PageServer? pagename=about_publications_justdiag> (September 30, 2009).

2. Mayo Foundation for Medical Education and Research, *Mayo Clinic On Depression: Answers to Help You Understand, Recognize, and Manage Depression*, 1st ed., ed. Keith Kramlinger, MD (Rochester, Minn.: MayoClinic Health Information, 2001), pp. 88–91.

3. Patient composite is drawn from interviews with psychiatrists who are attending physicians at medical centers in New Jersey and New York (March—July 2008).

4. Mayo Foundation for Medical Education and Research, pp. 88–91.

5. Ibid.

6. Michael H. Ebert, MD, Peter T. Loosen, MD, Barry Nurcombe, MD, *Current Diagnosis and Treatment in Psychiatry* (New York: Lange Medical Books/ McGraw-Hill, 2000), pp. 33–36.

7. Anna Moore, "Eternal Sunshine: Anna Moore Looks at the History of Prozac," *The Guardian*, May 13, 2007, <http://www.guardian.co.uk/ society/2007/ may/13/socialcare.medicineandhealth/print> (September 30, 2009).

8. Depression and Bipolar Support Alliance.

9. Ibid.

10. Bruce Bower, "Prescription for controversy: medications for depressed kids spark scientific dispute," *Science News*, March 2006, <http://www.thefreelibrary.com/Prescription+for+controversy:+medications+ for+depressed+kids+spark...-a0144764150> (September 30, 2009).

11. Patient composite is drawn from interviews with psychiatrists who are attending physicians at medical centers in New Jersey and New York (March—July 2008).

12. Personal correspondence with David M.N. Paperny, FAAP, FSAM, December 2008.

13. Ibid.

14. National Institute of Mental Health, "Mental Health Medications," September 17, 2009, <http://www.nimh.nih.gov/health/publications/mental-health-medications/complete-index.shtml> (September 30, 2009).

15. Ronald R. Fieve, MD, *Moodswing*, 2nd ed., rev. (New York: Bantam Books, 1989), pp. 235–236.

16. National Institute of Mental Health, "Science Update: Properly Timed Light, Melatonin Lift Winter Depression by Syncing Rhythms," May 1, 2006, <http://www.nimh.nih.gov/science-news/2006/properly-timed-light-melatonin-lift-winter-depression-by-syncing-rhythms.shtml> (September 30, 2009).

17. Ibid.

18. Jen C. Wang, et al., "Evidence of common and specific genetic effects: association of the muscarinic acetylcholine receptor M2 (CHRM2) gene with alcohol dependence and major depressive syndrome," *Human Molecular Genetics*, September 1, 2004, pp. 1903–1911.

19. Ibid.

20. MedHelp, "All About Lithium," n.d., <http://www.medhelp.org/lib/ lithium.htm> (September 30, 2009).

21. Ibid.

22. Ibid.

23. Ibid.

24. Ibid.

25. David J. Milkowitz, *The Bipolar Disorder Survival Guide* (New York: The Guilford Press, 2002) pp. 104–110.

26. University of Pittsburg Medical Center News Bureau, "University of Pittsburgh Study Results Published in Archives of General Psychiatry," September 6, 2005, <http://www.pendulum.org/bpnews/archive/001769.html> (September 30, 2009).

27. Roger Granet, MD and Elizabeth Ferber, *Why Am I Up, Why Am I Down: Understanding Bipolar Disorder* (New York: Dell Books, 1999), p. 195.

28. Ibid.

29. Paul Forsyth, "Orthomolecular Medicine: Can Vitamins Help Those that Medication has Failed?" *National Alliance on Mental Illness*, Spring 2008, <http://www.nami.org/Template.cfm?Section=Schizophrenia&template=/Content Management/ContentDisplay.cfm&ContentID=60920> (September 30, 2009).

Chapter 6: Living With Depression and Bipolar Disorder

1. David J. Milkowitz, *The Bipolar Disorder Survival Guide* (New York: The Guilford Press, 2002), p. 226.

2. Lizzie Simon, *Detour: My Bipolar Road Trip in 4-D* (New York: Washington Square Press, 2002), p. 36.

3. Ibid.

4. Mental Health America, "10 Tips for Improving Family Mental Health," November 8, 2006, <http://www.mentalhealthamerica.net/go/information/get-info/ten-tips/10-tips-for-improving-family-mental-health> (September 30, 2009).

5. The National Sleep Foundation, "Depression and Sleep," n.d., <http://sleepfoun-dation.org/article/sleep-topics/depression-and-sleep> (September 30, 2009).

6. Ibid.

7. Charles W. Hoge, MD, et al., "Combat Duty in Iraq and Afghanistan, Mental Health Problems, and Barriers to Care," *The New England Journal of Medicine*, July 1, 2004, Vol. 351, pp. 13–22 <http://content.nejm.org/cgi/content/full/351/1/13> (September 30, 2009).

8. Ibid.

9. Mental Health America, "Mental Health America: Operation Healthy Reunions—Information for the troops and their families," n.d., <http://www.mentalhealthamerica.net/reunions/infoPTSD.cfm> (September 30, 2009).

10. Francis Mark Mondimore, MD, *Bipolar Disorder: A Guide for Patients and Families* (Baltimore: Johns Hopkins University Press, 1999), p. 240.

11. Ibid.

12. Herbert Benson, MD, Eileen M. Stuart, RN, *The Wellness Book* (New York: Simon & Schuster, 1992), p.137.

13. Mental Health America, "Factsheet: Coping With Stress Checklist," n.d., <http://www.mentalhealthamerica.net/go/information/get-info/stress/coping-with-stress-checklist/coping-with-stress-checklist> (October 20, 2009).

14. Gabrielle Glaser, "'Mad Pride' Fights a Stigma," *The New York Times*, May 11, 2008, pp. 1–2.

15. National Institute of Mental Health, "The Numbers Count: Mental Disorders in America," 2008, <http://www.nimh.nih.gov/health/publications/the-numbers-count-mental-disorders-in-america/index.shtml> (September 30, 2009).

16. Ibid.

17. Patricia Cohen, "Midlife Suicide Rate Rises, Puzzling Researchers," *The New York Times*, February 19, 2008, <http://www.nytimes.com/2008/02/19/us/19suicide.html?_r=1day2008> (September 30, 2009).

18. National Depressive and Manic Depressive Association, *Suicide and Depressive Illness* (Chicago: NDMDA, 1996), p. 17.

19. Harvard Medical School Office of Public Affairs, News Release: "Harvard Medical School Launches Division to Study Complementary Medicine," July 11, 2008, <http://www.bidmc.org/News/AroundBIDMC/2000/July/HarvardMedicalSchool LaunchesDivisiontoStudyComplementaryMedicine.aspx> (September 30, 2009).

20. National Depressive and Manic Depressive Association, p. 17.

21. Depression is Real Coalition, podcast, "The Up and Down Show," Show #16: "Suicide Prevention," March 16, 2008, <http://www.depressionisreal.org> (September 30, 2009).

22. National Depressive and Manic Depressive Association, p. 26.

23. Ibid.

24. Milkowitz, pp. 104–110.

25. Brightfutures.org, "Bright Futures in Practice: Mental Health—Volume II, Tool Kit, Bright Futures—at Georgetown," January 22, 2007, <http://www.brightfutures.org/mentalhealth/pdf/tools.html> (September 30, 2009).

26. Mayo Foundation for Medical Education and Research, *The Mayo Clinic on Depression*, ed., Keith Kramlinger, MD (Rochester: Mayo Clinic Health Information, 2001), pp. 54–57.

27. Ibid.

28. Mauro Geovanni Carta, "Improving physical quality of life with group physical adjunctive treatment of major depressive disorder," *Clinical Practices of Epidemiological Mental Health*, Vol. 4, 2008.

Chapter 7: When Someone You Love Has Depression or Bipolar Disorder

1. Kay Redfield Jamison, *An Unquiet Mind* (New York: Vintage Books, 1995), p. 75.

2. Patient composite is drawn from interviews with psychiatrists who are attending physicians at medical centers in New Jersey and New York (March—July 2008).

3. Ibid.

4. Patient composite is drawn from interviews with psychiatrists who are attending physicians at medical centers in New Jersey and New York (March—July 2008).

5. Pathways2promise.org, "Impact of Mental Illness on Families," n.d., <http://www.pathways2promise.org/family/impact.htm> (September 30, 2009).

6. Ibid.

7. Charles Atkins, MD, *The Bipolar Disorder Answer Book: Answers to More than 275 of Your Most Pressing Questions* (Naperville, Ill.: Sourcebooks, 2007), p. 260.

8. Francis Mark Mondimore, MD, *Bipolar Disorder: A Guide for Patients and Families* (Baltimore: The Johns Hopkins University Press, 1999), p. 240.

9. Peter J. Weiden, MD, "Should You Take the NAMI Family-to-Family Course?" December 16, 2000, <http://www.nami.org> (September 30, 2009).

10. Atkins, p. 260.

11. Pathways2promise.org.

12. Atkins, p. 260.

13. Mayo Foundation for Medical Education and Research, *The Mayo Clinic on Depression*, 1st ed., ed. Keith Kramlinger, MD (Rochester: Mayo Clinic Health Information, 2001), pp. 106–110.

14. Atkins, p. 260.

15. Ibid.

Chapter 8: Outlook for the Future

1. McLean Hospital, "Identification of Genes Provides New Clues into the Causes of Schizophrenia and Bipolar Disorder," June 4, 2007, <http://www.mclean.harvard.edu/news/press/current.php?id=109> (September 30, 2009).

2. Ibid.

3. Harvard Department of Psychiatry, "Cambridge Hospital Bipolar Disorder Research Program," n.d., <http://medapps.med.harvard.edu/psych/redbook/redbook-affectivedisorders-04.htm> (September 30, 2009).

4. Jean Frazier, MD, et al., "Brain Anatomic Magnetic Resonance Imaging in Childhood Bipolar Disorder," July 1996, <http://www.ncbi.nlm.nih.gov/pubmed/8660128> (September 30, 2009).

5. Sciencedaily.com, "History Of Depression Linked To More Brain Plaques And Tangles, Rapid Decline In Alzheimer's Disease," February 8, 2006, <http://www.sciencedaily.com/releases/2006/02/060206232204.htm> (September 30, 2009).

6. National Institute of Mental Health, "Statistics: The Impact of Mental Illness on Society," August 6, 2009, <http://www.nimh.nih.gov/health/topics/statistics/index.shtml> (September 30, 2009).

7. U.S. Public Health Service, "Overview of Cultural Diversity and Mental Health Services," n.d., <http://www.surgeongeneral.gov/library/mentalhealth/chapter2/sec8.html> (September 30, 3009).

8. Ibid.

9. Norma Ware, PhD, et al., "Connectedness and Citizenship: Redefining Social Integration," *Psychiatric Services*, April 2007, Vol. 58, no. 4, pp. 469–473.

10. Alan Schwarz, "Concussions Tied to Depression in Ex-N.F.L. Players," *The New York Times*, May 31, 2007, <http://www.nytimes.com/2007/05/31/sports/football/31concussions.html> (September 30, 3009).

11. U.S. Public Health Service.

12. Mark Thompson, "America's Medicated Army," *Time*, June 16, 2008, pp. 38–42.

13. Ibid.

Glossary

affective disorders—Sustained, disturbing emotional states; mood disorders.

anticonvulsants—Drugs prescribed primarily for seizure disorders that also can stabilize the mood swings of bipolar disorder.

antidepressant medications—Term for several categories of drugs in use since the 1970s to improve the symptoms of depression.

antipsychotic medications—Drugs typically prescribed for psychotic disorders, but also used for major cases of depression or bipolar disorder that are accompanied by hallucinations or delusions; in use since the early 1950s.

attention deficit hyperactivity disorder (ADHD)—A condition of irritability, impulsivity, and distractibility, with symptoms that frequently overlap with those of bipolar disorder, making accurate diagnosis difficult, especially at a young age.

bipolar disorder—A diagnostic term to describe patterns of abnormal and severe mood swings.

cognitive behavior therapy—Talk therapy that identifies unhealthy, negative beliefs and behaviors that contribute to depression, replacing them with healthy, positive ones.

coping skills—A set of positive problem-solving abilities enabling someone to find solutions to daily dilemmas.

delusions—False beliefs, such as the belief that one is God or Superman; a symptom of psychosis.

depression—A state of sustained, unhappy mood that persists for at least two weeks and typically includes lack of energy, problems with sleeping, loss of pleasure in hobbies and other activities, loss of concentration, and loss of appetite.

Diagnostic and Statistical Manual of Mental Disorders (DSM)—A reference text for psychiatrists that groups observable behaviors into diagnostic categories for the purpose of treating mental illness.

dysthymia—A consistent depressed state that lasts for years, but does not meet the diagnostic criteria of major depression.

electroconvulsive therapy—Treatment that involves the administration of electricity to cause seizures, or convulsions, which can relieve the symptoms of major depression.

endorphins—Brain chemicals that produce feelings of satisfaction and well-being.

estrogen—A female hormone that is linked to mood and depression, among its other functions.

euphoria—Another word for mania, a state of elevated mood; a symptom of bipolar disorder.

grief—A normal and necessary response to a significant loss, as opposed to major depression, which is long-lasting and can arise independent of any external event.

group therapy—Therapy involving a group of unrelated people and a mental health professional who work together toward the common goal of moving toward greater insight.

hallucinations—Often accompanying a state of psychosis, hallucinations are the perception of things that don't exist through one of the five senses; for example, an auditory hallucination involves hearing the voices of people who aren't there.

hypomania—A less intense form of mania.

hypothalamus—The part of the brain that regulates the body's response to stress.

inpatient hospitalization—Treatment that involves placing patients in the hospital as residents. They often stay in special wards or on floors where they can be observed and treated twenty-four hours a day.

insomnia—The inability to sleep normally; often a symptom of depression.

lamictal (lamotrigine)—A mood stabilizer prescribed for bipolar disorder.

light therapy—The use of artificially created full-spectrum light in the treatment of seasonal affective disorder (SAD).

limbic system—The part of the brain that processes and responds to messages from the senses and is involved in the regulation of mood and emotion.

lithium—A naturally occurring element (a salt) that is used as a mood stabilizer in the treatment of manic depression.

major depression—A mood change that lasts for more than two weeks and includes overwhelming feelings of sadness or grief and loss of interest in usually pleasurable activities.

manic depression—An older term for bipolar disorder.

manic episode—A sustained period of abnormally elevated mood.

medicare—A U.S. government health care plan that pays for certain medical expenses for people over age sixty-five.

melancholia—Depression, usually not severe but sometimes repetitive.

mixed episode—A type of bipolar mood state in which symptoms of both mania and depression are present at the same time.

monoamine oxidase inhibitors (MAOIs)—A type of antidepressant medication that is highly effective, but is rarely prescribed because of its side effects.

mood charts—Journals that follow the course of mood and include mood state, medications taken, energy level, and (for women) menstrual cycles.

mood stabilizers—Medications that even out the highs and lows of bipolar disorder.

negative thinking—A pattern of unhealthy thought in which someone always expects the worst to happen.

neurotransmitters—Chemical messengers that transfer information between nerve cells.

norepinephrine—A type of neurotransmitter.

outpatient treatment—Hospital and clinic-based programs for psychiatric patient that offer daytime therapy, support groups, training programs, and other services to integrate patients back into a productive and healthy life.

postpartum depression—A major depression caused by the sudden hormonal changes that follow the birth of a child.

post-traumatic stress disorder (PTSD)—A psychological and emotional condition that affects people who have lived through a terrible event such as war, a rape, or a natural disaster.

psychiatrist—A medical doctor specializing in mental, emotional or behavioral disorders.

psychoanalysis—An intense psychological evaluation and treatment regimen developed by Sigmund Freud, based on the idea that talking about conflicts helps to heal them and bring insight to patients.

psychologist—A professional with a PhD who specializes in the treatment of emotional disorders, research about them, or both.

psychosis—A state of mind characterized by delusions, hallucinations, and nonsensical thoughts.

schizophrenia—A condition characterized by psychotic symptoms such as delusions, hallucinations, and disorganized thoughts.

seasonal affective disorder (SAD)—A form of depression caused by the shortening days of fall/winter and the lessening of sunlight, both of which affect chemical changes in the brain.

selective serotonin reuptake inhibitors (SSRIs)—A type of antidepressant medication that came into widespread use in the 1980s and is considered the most effective category of antidepressants with the fewest side effects.

suicide—The taking of one's own life, often caused by untreated or inadequately treated depression.

tricyclic antidepressants—The first generation of antidepressant medication, in widespread use in the 1970s.

unipolar depression—Depression characterized by one feeling state—sadness—as opposed to bipolar depression, which is characterized by a cycle of moods.

valproic acid—A category of medication originally developed to treat epilepsy and now used as a mood stabilizer to control the mood shifts of bipolar disorder.

For More Information

Further Reading

Atkins, Charles, MD. *The Bipolar Disorder Answer Book: Answers to More Than 275 of Your Most Pressing Questions.* Naperville, Ill.: Sourcebooks, Inc., 2007.

Cobain, Bev. *When Nothing Matters Anymore: A Survival Guide for Depressed Teens.* Minneapolis, Minn: Free Spirit Publishing, 2007.

Jamieson, Patrick E., and Moira A. Rynn. *Mind Race: A Firsthand Account of One Teenager's Experience With Bipolar Disorder.* Oxford, N.Y.: Oxford University Press, 2006.

Miller, Allen R. *Living With Depression.* New York: Facts on File, 2007.

Monaque, Mathilde. *Trouble in My Head: A Young Girl's Fight with Depression.* New York: Random House, 2007.

Internet Addresses

Mental Health America. © 1995–2008. <http://www.nmha.org>

National Mental Health Information Center. © 2008. <http://www.healthfinder.gov>

Organizations

American Academy of Child and Adolescent Psychiatry
3613 Wisconsin Avenue, N.W.
Washington, DC 20016
(202) 966-7300
<http://www.aacap.org>

American Foundation for Suicide Prevention
120 Wall Street, 22nd Floor
New York, NY 10005
(888) 333-2377
<http://www.afsp.org>

American Psychiatric Association
1400 K Street, N.W.
Washington, DC 20005
(888) 357-7924
<http://www.psych.org>

National Alliance for the Mentally Ill
3 Colonial Place
2107 Wilson Blvd., Suite 300
Arlington, VA 22201
(703) 524-7600
Help Line: (800) 950-NAMI (6264)
<http://www.nami.org>

National Depressive and Manic Depressive Association
730 North Franklin Street, Suite 501
Chicago, IL 60610
(800) 826-3632
<http://www.ndmda.org>

National Institute of Mental Health
NIMH Public Inquiries
6001 Executive Blvd., Room 8186
Bethesda, MD 20892
(301) 443-4513
<http://www.nimh.nih.gov>

National Mental Health Association
1021 Prince Street
Alexandria, VA 22314
(800) 969-6642
<http://www.nmha.org>

Index